INSTRUCTOR'S RESOURCE MANUAL

DISCOVERING THE WESTERN PAST

INSTRUCTOR'S RESOURCE MANUAL

DISCOVERING THE WESTERN PAST

A LOOK AT THE EVIDENCE
Second Edition

Merry E. Wiesner

University of Wisconsin—Milwaukee

Julius R. Ruff

Marquette University

William Bruce Wheeler

University of Tennessee, Knoxville

Houghton Mifflin Company   Boston   Toronto

Dallas   Geneva, Illinois   Palo Alto   Princeton, New Jersey

Sponsoring Editor: Sean W. Wakely
Senior Development Editor: Lance Wickens
Senior Project Editor: Carol Newman
Senior Production/Design Coordinator: Martha Drury
Electronic Publishing Specialist: Claire Hollenbeck
Senior Manufacturing Coordinator: Marie Barnes
Marketing Manager: Becky Dudley

Printed in the U.S.A.

ISBN: 0-395-63901-8

123456789-B–96 95 94 93 92

Contents

Preface

The success of the first edition of *Discovering the Western Past: A Look at the Evidence* encouraged us to undertake a second edition of the book. In this revision every chapter has received some attention, and a number of chapters have been rewritten entirely. Nevertheless, our goals remain the same as they were in the first edition: to convey to undergraduate students the exciting variety of sources and methodologies available to the historian for studying the past.

As historians and as teachers of history, all of us in the field approach the past in individual ways. Our sources and methodology vary tremendously, and so do the conclusions we draw about causation and historical significance. Communicating (and validating) this diversity was one of the main reasons for compiling *Discovering the Western Past: A Look at the Evidence*. Another important reason was to give students the opportunity to "do history" themselves, to analyze evidence and to come to conclusions on their own in the same way we as historians do. Including an *Instructor's Resource Manual* with the text may at first glance seem to belie these intentions, placing us as authors and you as the instructor back in the role of the authority who provides the "right" answers. Because this is not what we want to do, we have written a manual that differs in significant ways from those that usually accompany Western Civilization textbooks. You will find no multiple-choice or true-false questions but rather suggestions on how to assist your students as they learn various analytical and interpretive skills and solve historical problems.

Each chapter follows the format of the book itself, beginning with a general introduction to the topic. For the section called The Problem, we have set out some specific content and skills objectives for the evidence presented in that chapter. These lists should not be regarded as exhaustive; skills such as critical reading and analyzing arguments may be learned and practiced in every chapter. We have also provided some ideas about ways in which the discussion provoked by the chapter could be broadened by introducing comparative issues or more speculative and philosophical concerns. We have intentionally limited the number of direct parallels to modern situations in the student text, including them here instead and leaving to your discretion the amount of time you want to devote to modern comparisons. This section also includes ideas on some of the ways in which various chapters could be connected.

In the Sources and Method section, we discuss how we have introduced the chapter in our own classes, noting the additional contextual or methodological background we have found necessary to provide. Because Western Civilization textbooks vary so tremendously in the space they devote to certain issues, you may find either that some of this supplementary material is unnecessary or that even more background is needed. The amount of methodological support you will need to provide depends both on the type of evidence in the chapter and on the sophistication of your students. We have tried to indicate those chapters most students should be able to tackle independently; you may decide to assign these for out-of-class work, reserving chapters in which students will probably need help for more extensive classroom coverage. The Evidence section identifies those sources that may need specific discussion and suggests ways of guiding students as they piece information together from the different sources.

Though it may seem that the Questions to Consider section in the student text examines the chapter's topic from every possible angle, we have included more questions in the corresponding section here, particularly those that may stimulate your students to think about the larger implications of their discoveries. In the Epilogue and Evaluation sections of this manual, we have made some suggestions about ways in which student mastery of each chapter may be evaluated. These include traditional forms of evaluation such as graded discussions, essay examination questions, and writing assignments based on the chapter as well as innovative techniques such as classroom debates and rewriting the textbook. In addition, we have suggested ways in which the chapter could serve as a springboard to broader research or comparative projects. Each chapter in the *Instructor's Resource Manual* ends with a brief list of suggestions for further reading, including works of interest to students and instructors alike.

Throughout this manual we have tried to indicate why we chose the focus we did in each chapter and why we regard that historical issue as significant and interesting. Because nothing varies more among historians than just this—what they consider significant or interesting—we hope above all that the variety of sources and methods included here will help you communicate that diversity of outlook to your students. If the second edition of *Discovering the Western Past* enables you to explain in greater depth both how and why we "do history," and if your students experience some of the fascination with the past that we as professional historians share, then we will have succeeded in our aims.

M.E.W.   J.R.R.   W.B.W.

Discovering the Western Past and Your Text

Discovering the Western Past: A Look at the Evidence is intended to accompany any Western Civilization text that you select. Moreover, each chapter is self-contained, so that any combination of chapters may be assigned. To help you supplement your text effectively with our book, the charts on pages xi and xii directly relate Volumes I and II of *Discovering the Western Past* to seventeen popular Western Civilization textbooks, listed below. The charts are easily read: textbook chapters linked in content to our book are listed beneath the appropriate chapters in Volumes I and II.

Remember that the charts present only obvious parallels; as we suggest in this manual, many chapters in *Discovering the Western Past* echo others in content or methodology, allowing you to broaden classroom discussions or assignments as desired.

Textbooks

Chambers, Mortimer; Grew, Raymond; Herlihy, David; Rabb, Theodore K.; and Woloch, Isser. *The Western Experience*, 5th ed. Vol. I: *To 1715*; Vol. II: *Since 1600*. New York: McGraw-Hill, 1991.

Chodorow, Stanley; Knox, MacGregor; Schirokauer, Conrad; Strayer, Joseph R.; and Gatzke, Hans W. *The Mainstream of Civilization*, 5th ed. Vol. I: *To 1785*; Vol. II: *Since 1660*. San Diego: Harcourt Brace Jovanovich, 1989.

Goff, Richard D.; Cassar, George H.; Esler, Anthony; Holoka, James P.; and Waltz, James C. *A Survey of Western Civilization*. 2 vols. St. Paul: West, 1987.

Greer, Thomas H.; and Lewis, Gavin. *A Brief History of the Western World*, 6th ed. San Diego: Harcourt Brace Jovanovich, 1992.

Harrison, John B.; Sullivan, Richard E.; and Sherman, Dennis. *A Short History of Western Civilization*, 7th ed. New York: McGraw-Hill, 1990.

Kagan, Donald; Ozment, Steven; and Turner, Frank M. *The Western Heritage*, 4th ed. Vol. I: *To 1715*; Vol.II: *Since 1648*. New York: Macmillan, 1991.

Kishlansky, Mark; Geary, Patrick; and O'Brien, Patricia. *Civilization in the West*. New York: Harper Collins, 1991.

Lerner, Robert E.; Meachem, Standish; and Burns, Edward McNall. *Western Civilizations: Their History and Their Culture*, 11th ed. 2 vols. New York: Norton, 1988.

McKay, John P.; Hill, Bennett D.; and Buckler, John. *A History of Western Society*, 4th ed. Vol I: *From Antiquity to the Enlightenment*; Vol. II: *From Absolutism to the Present*. Boston: Houghton Mifflin, 1991.

McNeill, William H. *History of Western Civilization: A Handbook*, 6th ed. Chicago: University of Chicago Press, 1986.

Palmer, R. R.; and Colton, Joel. *A History of the Modern World*, 7th ed. Vol. I: *To 1815*; Vol. II: *Since 1815*. New York: McGraw-Hill, 1991.

Perry, Marvin; Chase, Myrna; Jacob, James R.; Jacob, Margaret C.; and Von Laue, Theodore H. *Western Civilization: Ideas, Politics, and Society*, 4th ed. Boston: Houghton Mifflin, 1992.

Spielvogel, Jackson J. *Western Civilization*. Vol. I: *To 1715*; Vol. II: *Since 1550*. St. Paul: West, 1991.

Wallbank, T. Walter; Taylor, Alastair M.; Bailkey, Nels M.; Jewsbury, George F.; Lewis, Clyde J.; and Hackett, Neil J. *Civilization Past and Present*, 7th ed. Vol. I: *To 1714*; Vol. II: *Since 1648*. New York: Harper Collins, 1991.

Willis, F. Roy. *Western Civilization*, 4th ed. Vol. I: *From Ancient Times Through the Seventeenth Century*; Vol. II: *From the Seventeenth Century Through the Contemporary Age*. Lexington, Mass.: D. C. Heath, 1985.

Willis, F. Roy. *Western Civilization: A Brief Introduction*. New York: Macmillan, 1987.

Winks, Robin W.; Brinton, Crane; Christopher, John B.; and Wolff, Robert Lee. *A History of Civilization*, 8th ed. Vol I: *Prehistory to 1715*; Vol. II: *1648 to the Present*. Englewood Cliffs, N.J.: Prentice-Hall, 1992.

Discovering the Western Past, Volume I (by chapter)

	1	2	3	4	5	6	7	8	9	10	11	12	13	14
Chambers (chap.)	1–5	3	5	5–6	8	8	8	9	9	11	12	13	14	14
Chodorow	1–4	2	4	4–5	10	9	10	11	11	11	16	18	17	17
Goff	1–9	2–4	7	9–10	15	15	14	12	12	13	18	19	20	19
Greaves	1–5	2	4–5	5	7	7	8	7	7	8–9	10	12	11	15
Greer	1–3	2	3	4	5	5	6	5, 7	7	6	8	7	9	10
Harrison	1–11	4–5	10	15	20	17	23	18	18	22	26–27	29	30	32
Kagen	1–5	3	5	6	7	6	8	8	8	9	10	10	11	13
Kishlansky	1–6	3	5	6	8	9	9	9	9	10	11	12	13	16
Lerner	1–7	5	7	8	10	10	11	10	10	11	13	14	14	17
McKay	1–6	3	6	7	9	9	11	11	11	11	13	15	14	16
McNeill	IA, IIC–D	IIA	IID	IIF	IIIB2	IIIB2	IIIB2	IIIB2	IIIB2	IIIB3	IIIB3	IIIB3	IIIC1	IIIC2
Palmer	1	1	1	1	1	1	1	1	1	1	2	2	3	4
Perry	1, 3–7	3	7	8	10	10	11	10	10	12	13	15	14	16
Spielvogel	1–6	3	6	7	9	8	10	11	11	12	13	15	14	16
Wallbank	1–3	2	3	5	8	10	11	9	9	11	13	18	14	
Willis	1–4	2	4	5	8	7	9	8	8	10	11	13	12	15
Willis, brief	1–3	2	3	4	6	5	6	6	6	7	7	9	8	10
Winks	1–3	2	3	4	8	5	7	7	7	7	11	14	12	15

Discovering the Western Past, Volume II (by chapter)

	1	2	3	4	5	6	7	8	9	10	11	12	13	14	15
Chambers (chap.)		17	19	20	20	23	25	23	26	27	26	26	28	30	30
Chodorow		20	21	22	23	24	25	24	27	28	30	30	32	34	36
Goff		22	24	22	27	29	30	29	36	35, 40	38	42	42	46	46
Greaves		15	18	17	19	20	21	23	24	25	26	27	27	30	30
Greer	9	10	10	10	11	12	12	12	13	15	13	13	13	14	14
Harrison		32	38	36	40	44	43	44	49	52	53	54	55	58	58
Kagen		13	18	16	19	22	22	24	26	25	26	26	28	31	31
Kishlansky	13	16	19	19	20	21	22	24	25	24	26	26	28	29	30
Lerner		17	18	16	19	21	22	21	24	25	27	27	28	30	31
McKay		16	18	20	21	22	23	24, 25	26	28	27	27	29	32	32
McNeill	IIIC1	IIIC2	IIIC2	IIIC2	IIIC2	IIIC3	IIIC3	IIIC3	IIIC3	111C3	IIIC4	IIIC4	IIIC4	IIIC4	IIIC4
Palmer															
Perry		16	18	18	19	21	22, 24	26	27	28	30	31	32	35	36
Spielvogel		16	18	19	20	21	22, 23	24	25	25	26	26	27	29	29
Wallbank		19	21	22	23	25	25	25	27	31	30	30	32	36, 37	36
Willis		15	16	16	17	19	19	21	20	21	22	23	24	26	26
Willis, brief	8	10	11	12	13	14	14	17	18	20	18	19	19	21	21
Winks		15	17	16	18	20	20	20	22	27	23	23	24	28	28

INSTRUCTOR'S RESOURCE MANUAL

DISCOVERING THE WESTERN PAST

CHAPTER ONE

The Need for Water in Ancient Societies

Many Western Civilization courses begin by examining the cultural and religious development of ancient Near Eastern societies, asking students to read sources such as the Egyptian *Hymn to the Sun* or the *Epic of Gilgamesh*. We have found that students have very little sense of basic patterns of life in any premodern society and so are unable to put these documents into context. It is difficult for them to understand, for example, why the sun was so important to the Egyptians or why Gilgamesh feels himself at the mercy of the gods and not in control of his fate. By focusing on water, the most important resource in any agricultural society, this chapter provides an environmental context within which early political, cultural, and technological developments can be more fully understood. Water as an issue also links ancient societies with today's world, helping students to gain familiarity with an early period by identifying a common problem that has existed throughout human history.

The Problem

All the chapters in *Discovering the Western Past* have two sets of objectives: one set relating to content, the other to skills. Your role as an instructor will be not only to ensure that students grasp the material and learn the history they should from the chapter but also to help them gain skills in reading, analyzing, and discussing. Objectives for "The Need for Water in Ancient Societies" follow.

Content objectives:

1. to learn how irrigation and water supply systems work

2. to understand how technological problems were solved before the invention of modern machinery

3. to see the relations among technological, legal, and political change

4. to realize that ancient societies were not "primitive" but highly complex social organizations

Skills objectives:

1. to examine visual evidence carefully, noting small details

2. to visualize from a written description

3. to combine visual and written sources to address a historical problem

Along with these fairly specific objectives, you may wish to use this chapter to stimulate discussion of some of the following broader questions:

1. How do political decisions affect the distribution of resources? In turn, how does a scarcity of some basic resource contribute to the growth of political power among the groups or individuals that control the resources?

2. Why would people who had once enjoyed the benefits of irrigation allow ditches to silt in and the system to become unusable?

3. Besides water, what other resources in the modern world are essential to civilization? (The most obvious answer to this question is oil, and it may be fruitful in discussion to compare the way the need for oil has shaped modern culture to the way the need for water shaped ancient civilization. Using the oil crisis as a parallel may enable students to see political and economic connections more clearly.)

4. The need for a regular supply of water was created by settled agriculture and large concentrations of people living in cities; hunter-gatherers do not usually build irrigation ditches. What sorts of conflicts might emerge as agriculturalists began to move into areas populated by hunter-gatherers, as was the case in southern and central Europe?

These are, of course, not the only possible questions that emerge from this chapter. You may also wish to use this topic as a springboard for an even more far-ranging discussion of the nature of "civilization" or "progress."

Sources and Method

Although much has been made of the difficulty many students have in reading, we have found that they also have difficulty in examining visual evidence. Students often skip over illustrations and diagrams in textbooks, or give them only a cursory glance, because they regard the written text as all that matters. You may want to spend part of the class time discussing why visual evidence is so important in studying the earliest periods of human history. You may also want to ask students to think about the nature of the evidence we have left, stressing the differences between those materials, such as stone and bone, that survive and others, such as hides and clothing, that generally do not. This would also be a good time to discuss carbon-14 dating and other methods used by paleontologists and historians to date the objects they find. You might stress the limitations of archaeological evidence: ask students to think about the sorts of information that can never be known about a society if all that survives of it are archaeological remains. This discussion can be a good springboard into the subject of the importance of written records as a source of historical evidence.

The written evidence in this chapter may be quite technical for some students, though many will see it as refreshingly straightforward because it is primarily descriptive. If students are having trouble visualizing from the written material how irrigation systems work, you might ask them to draw a diagram of, for instance, the Roman aqueduct system. This will also encourage them to think about technical obstacles to construction such as valleys and hills. This method can help with the visual evidence as well; for example, if students cannot easily see how the water-lifting machines work, ask them to trace the course of the water as it passes through these machines.

Because this chapter includes material from both ancient Mesopotamia and Rome, you may wish to include some information on the political organization of both areas in your introduction. This will reinforce the point that the distribution of water was both a political and a technological problem, as well as clarify why the Roman emperors and not some lesser functionaries built the aqueducts and set out the laws for the distribution of water.

Because so much of the information about premodern societies survives as legal codes rather than actual court records, this is a good place to talk about the limitations inherent in using law codes as historical evidence. The text notes that laws are often reissued when the activity they are attempting to prohibit continues, and it would be useful for you to reinforce this point in classroom discussion as well. You may also wish to expand on the differences between prescriptive and descriptive sources because that distinction, so vital for students to grasp, will emerge again in several other chapters.

The Evidence

To answer the questions posed about the visual evidence, students must notice various details. Most of these they will pick up without your prompting, but occasionally some leading questions can help. In Source 1, they need to be aware that the flatness of the landscape would lead to silt buildup and the need for water-lifting machines if farmers wanted perennial irrigation. (There is no drop in elevation that would make water flow through these ditches by gravity.) The LANDSAT image demonstrates the size and complexity of the Mesopotamian system, making it clear that irrigation ditches were not found simply on the outskirts of cities but also in the lands between them. This should lead students to see that a state of constant hostility between cities in Mesopotamia would not have been conducive to effective irrigation because the Tigris and Euphrates are the only actual sources of water and many cities were located far from them. (The small triangles are the sites of major ancient cities.) To reinforce the connections between irrigation and the growth of centralized political power, you could refer to this map later when you discuss the development of Greece, which did not have large irrigation systems and did experience fairly constant hostility between cities.

The text asks the students to make a chart of the advantages and disadvantages in each of the water-lifting machines. The long string of questions should guide their assessments, but you can assist them in recognizing the positive and negative points of each machine: the shaduf lifts only a small amount of water and needs constant human attendance, but it is a very simple device that does not need to be made of metal. (You may need to point out that metal was a luxury commodity in ancient societies; also, raw ore and skill at smelting were not available everywhere. Like water, metals are a resource whose distribution is determined by natural, technological, and political factors alike; this distribution could in turn have political consequences. For example, the power of the Egyptian pharaohs declined when iron replaced bronze as the most important metal for weapons and tools because Egypt had no iron, though it did have large copper mines.) The saqiya is more complicated and requires an animal to operate, but it can be overseen by a child rather than the strong adult needed to operate the shaduf. The saqiya can also lift water out of wells, whereas the other machines are useful only for rivers and ditches. The Archimedes' screw requires constant labor and can lift water only a short distance; however, because water flows through it continuously, this device lifts much more than the shaduf in the same amount of time. The noria, the most complex of the machines, needs flowing water to operate; on the positive side, it does not require either human attendance or animal power.

Turning to the written sources, the text asks the students to distinguish the technical, legal, political, and economic issues involved in the distribution of water. These should be fairly straightforward, but students may need your assistance first in separating these issues and then in discerning their inter-connections. In discussing the selection from the Code of Hammurabi, you may wish to mention other parts of the code not presented here that also pro-vide stiff punishments for various infractions. It is important to point out that even though Hammurabi's penalties may seem draconian to us, in western Europe as late as the eighteenth century people could be hanged or deported for stealing a handkerchief. Section 54 of the Code of Hammurabi notes that if someone neglects his dike, "they shall sell him and his goods." This seems a logical place to discuss slavery for debt in the ancient world and even the nature of ancient slavery in general. (Students tend to think all slavery is ra-cial or the result of war.)

In discussing the Roman aqueducts, it may be interesting for students to learn that the system was so large that it is the first known example of a stan-dardization of components. At the time of Frontinus, the aqueduct system was supposed to be able to provide about 90 gallons per person per day. It is unlikely that the system ever provided quite that much, but Rome used more water per person than any other society until the advent of modern indoor plumbing.

Vitruvius's discussion of lead poisoning is a fascinating example of early awareness of environmental hazards. His sophisticated analysis led him to conclude that lead pipes were bad because the workers who produced lead became ill from contact with the metal. Lead poisoning is increasingly re-garded by historians as one of the many factors contributing to a decline in the Roman empire; Romans ingested lead not only from water pipes but also from lead cooking vessels and red lead that was intentionally mixed with pepper by unscrupulous merchants to increase its weight. Wealthier Romans ingested even more lead than poorer ones because of their prodigious con-sumption of wine, which was frequently mixed with a grape syrup that had been boiled down in leaded containers. The syrup enhanced the color and bouquet of the wine but contained so much lead that a teaspoon a day was enough to cause chronic lead poisoning.

Questions to Consider

This section encourages students to gather what they have learned from all the evidence and also poses some additional questions for discussion and speculation. You will probably need to reinforce the message of the text that speculation is an activity in which historians constantly engage, especially when they are examining ancient societies for which limited evidence sur-vives. It is also important for students to see that this speculation is based on concrete evidence, not simply flights of fancy. Too often students want to divide everything into mutually exclusive categories of "fact" and "opinion," with the former the domain of the sciences and the latter of the humanities. This chapter can help them see that historians' theories about the past are as squarely based on evidence as physicists' theories about the nature of the universe.

Some of the technological problems you may wish to discuss include: the difficulties of prospecting for ore to make pipes and fittings; building bridge supports; constructing pipes that fit together well enough to create the pressure needed to move the water over hills; keeping water pressure constant without the use of pumps; preserving wooden parts from rotting. Some of these problems still perplex hydraulic engineers. Many of the legal issues mentioned in the sources also continue to the present day, particularly illegal diversion of water by individuals. Numerous modern lawsuits, especially in the western United States, also charge communities and in some cases whole states with stealing the water that belongs to another area.

Students have obviously grasped the fact that an enormous amount of labor was needed to build and maintain these irrigation systems. Because some of this labor was provided by slaves, the evidence here can be integrated into a discussion of slavery in the ancient world. Because students probably have seen numerous bad movies of slaves building the pyramids, it is important to point out that most of this work was done not by slaves but by free individuals working for very low wages. The low value of labor in ancient societies is clear from the sources in this chapter, and this fact may help students to understand later in the course why the Athenians viewed a person who worked for wages as never able to be truly "free." The low cost of labor in ancient Rome probably worked against technological development because it meant there was no motivation for mechanization. You may wish to ask students to contrast this kind of society with the modern United States, in which industrial automation generally lowers the cost of production dramatically though it may also lead to higher rates of unemployment.

Epilogue and Evaluation

The epilogue first traces the fate of some of the ancient irrigation systems discussed in the chapter, then asks students to think about modern parallels to both the benefits and problems of irrigation. The Aswan Dam is cited as an example, but students are then asked to think about the current distribution of water in their own region. We have pointed out modern analogues at several points in this chapter, and you may wish either to save all these examples until students have completed their analysis of ancient society or to bring them up throughout the discussion. Along with the building of the Aswan Dam, the diversion of the Colorado River and the depletion of the Ogalalla Aquifer provide good modern comparative examples. You may wish to ask students to bring in newspaper or journal articles discussing current legal and political problems associated with the distribution of water or to look up the sections of local law codes that deal with such matters. In that way comparisons can be made not only between ancient and modern issues but also between ancient and modern sources.

There are a number of ways students may be evaluated in this chapter. The central question may be used as a written assignment or as an examination or quiz question. You may also wish to pose a counterfactual question along the lines of: "What would ancient societies have looked like if they hadn't been faced with the problem of irrigation?" You may also describe an imaginary society with a specific terrain, population density, social and economic structure, and governmental system, and then ask students to design an irrigation and water supply system for it. Once they have done this, they can be asked to assess the possible effects their system would have on the political, social, and economic structure of the society.

For Further Reading

Thomas Ashby, *The Aqueducts of Ancient Rome* (1973). An exhaustive survey of the building of each of the Roman aqueducts; covers both how they were built and how historians have learned about them.

Karl Butzer, *Early Hydraulic Civilization in Egypt* (1976). A discussion of both technical and political aspects of using the Nile for irrigation purposes.

Leo Deuel, *Flights into Yesterday: The Story of Aerial Archeology* (1969). Traces the history of the use of aerial photography for historical purposes. Somewhat romanticized, but fascinating reading and not too technical.

R. J. Forbes, *Studies in Ancient Technology* (1958–1965). A six-volume series offering comprehensive articles on a variety of topics.

Donald Hill, *A History of Engineering in Classical and Medieval Times* (1984). Examines not only irrigation and water-lifting machines but also dams, bridges, roads, surveying, and water and wind power. Excellent diagrams.

J. C. Landels, *Engineering in the Ancient World* (1978). Slightly more technical than Hill but fine for those who understand some engineering.

Norman A. F. Smith, *Man and Water* (1975). Surveys hydraulic techniques from prehistoric times to the present.

CHAPTER TWO

The Ideal and the Reality of Classical Athens

No period in the history of Western civilization has been held up as an ideal as often as classical Athens. The Italian Renaissance and the American Revolution often inspire similar encomiums, but because classical Athens served as a model during these periods, praising them reflects indirectly on the standard view of the "Golden Age" of Greece as well. Only during the past twenty years have historians, literary scholars, and art historians begun to reevaluate their sources to achieve a more balanced picture of the whole of Athenian society. This picture has disturbed more traditional scholars, some of whom have simply refused to accept what the sources quite clearly indicate, especially in regard to the status of women, the role of slaves, and the opinions of Socrates and Plato on democracy.

We have decided to tackle directly the issue of ideal versus reality in this chapter, not simply as a historiographic issue, but as an integral component of the very sources on which historians base their ideas. The conflict between the ideal and real has been a basic one in Western philosophy since Plato's time, but it is too often either presented as a very simple dichotomy ("Plato was an idealist and Aristotle a realist") or not covered because the subject is seen as too complex for most students to grasp, especially when it grows into the medieval Scholastic debate between realists and nominalists. We feel it is important for students to be able to grasp the distinction between ideal and reality when they read any source, and so we have chosen to emphasize this polarity early in the course. The central point of this chapter is one that you can return to in all later chapters and in any additional reading students are doing for the course.

The Problem

Content objectives:

1. to understand how Athenians in power saw their city and its role in history

2. to learn how Athens treated neighboring states

3. to examine a range of Athenian ideas about the position of slaves and women

4. to visualize the physical appearance of classical Athens

5. to learn how ideals of human conduct proposed by different Athenian thinkers varied from one social group to another

6. to examine the Athenian concept of democracy

Skills objectives:

1. to read critically, grasping the assumptions underlying an author's statements

2. to assess the relative value of both sides of a debate

3. to follow the ideas of each speaker in a dialogue

4. to analyze architectural plans

On a larger scale, you may want to introduce one or more of the following questions for discussion:

1. Do you think Pericles really believed what he was saying was true? If so, how do you account for the way the Athenians treated the Melians?

2. Why do you think Plato developed ideas about the role of women so different from those held by Pericles, Xenophon, and Aristotle?

3. Can you think of other historical periods in which a large gulf existed between social ideals and social reality? (The antebellum South may be one most familiar to students.)

4. Aristotle is often viewed as the champion of logical reasoning in Western philosophy. Do his ideas about the differences between women and men and between slaves and free men appear logical to you? Why might they have appeared logical to Aristotle and his contemporaries?

Most of these questions point to an even broader issue raised by this chapter: how can the ideals held about one's own society blind one to reality? For those who enjoy making comparisons with the current political and social scene, the opportunities are endless.

Sources and Method

Rather than simply instruct students to read and examine the sources, this chapter asks them to list the qualities that describe ancient Athens and the Athenians. This task is assigned not only to assist students in answering the central question but also to demonstrate how historians change their minds about an issue as they examine new sources. By crossing qualities off their list and adding new ones as they read, students refine their own ideas about classical Greece and also realize that generalizations about "Athens" are misleading when slaves, poorer people, and women had such a different experience of the "Golden Age." You may wish to extend this demonstration of how their picture of the classical world has been sharpened by asking your students to reread Pericles' speech once they have finished the chapter. By doing this, they can discover how the information they gain from a source is shaped by their own perspective. This exercise is particularly appropriate in this chapter, for most of the reevaluation of ancient Athens that has occurred in the past twenty years has come through the reexamination of already known sources from a fresh perspective rather than the discovery of substantial new evidence.

The chapter addresses the issue of distinguishing between ancient and modern primary sources, and you may wish to discuss this distinction further in your introduction. Though it may seem premature to discuss the impact of printing at this point, it is not too early to point out the problems associated with the survival of sources in a manuscript culture because this issue will recur in many of the subsequent chapters.

The textbook your students are using probably offers a discussion of political and military developments in ancient Athens adequate to provide a background for these sources. You may wish to emphasize the causes and outcome of the Peloponnesian War and the constant dispute between those who wanted to broaden Athenian democracy and those who wished to limit it. The conclusions students have drawn from the sources may also be used as a corrective for their textbooks. In its discussion of the democratic political party in Athens, for example, does their text mention that no free man in Athens ever contemplated extending representation to women or slaves? Is slavery, in fact, mentioned at all in the text, and if so, does the coverage seem adequate? Does the text make clear that about one-third of the Athenian population was slaves?

The Evidence

Students should have little problem reading and comprehending most of the written sources, though you may wish to bring out the fact that Sources 1 and 2 are parts of a work that is clearly history, Sources 3 and 6 are philosophical treatises, and Sources 4 and 5 are social commentary. Sources 1 and 2 include speeches or debates that Thucydides reports as if he had heard them in person, which, in the case of the Melian debate and perhaps Pericles' speech, he certainly had not. Though this fact troubles many readers because it appears as if Thucydides is inventing dialogue and action, he uses these speeches to allow historical figures to explain their aims and motivations. The speeches may not be literally accurate in the way they would in the era of tape recorders, but they represent Thucydides' best conjectures about why people acted the way they did. Thucydides thought that historians should not only record what had happened but also try to explain it, because he expected similar events to occur in the future and hoped people would learn from the mistakes of the past. Questions arising from Thucydides' use of speeches could lead to a broader discussion of the Greek cyclical view of history, ancient historians' ideas about historical accuracy, or differences among historians about the purpose of writing history.

Sources 5 and 6 are both dialogues, and students may need some assistance in following the flow of the conversation. In Source 5, Socrates serves more or less as a sounding board to Ischomachus, and most of the dialogue is actually a monologue. Source 6 is a true Socratic dialogue in which Plato makes his point by means of the questions that Socrates asks and the way he directs the conversation. The "I" in this dialogue is, of course, Socrates. You should probably explain that this is the way Plato wrote most of his works, and it is therefore difficult to distinguish his ideas from those of his mentor Socrates. Along with expressing Plato's thoughts on the ideal state, Source 6 can serve as introduction to Socrates' ideas about the process of learning and the nature of knowledge, for here Socrates clearly exhibits his characteristic method of questioning and his unwillingness to make dogmatic statements. You may wish to ask students to compare this approach to the forceful way Aristotle expresses his ideas and also to think about why Socrates' continual questioning might have annoyed many Athenians.

Sources 7 and 8 may require more guidance on your part than the written sources, because students have probably not thought about architecture or the organization of space as reflecting social ideals. To make this concept clearer, you may want to bring up more familiar examples, such as the post–World War II growth of suburbs full of single-family dwellings in the United States. In examining the diagrams themselves, you will want to make sure students notice that the women's quarters are in the rear of the house, separated from most of the rest of the house and the outside by a gate. This gate was often locked, and there was no door from the women's quarters leading directly outside. The agora serves as a physical demonstration of the fact that the male citizens thought all facets of their lives should be interconnected; religious, commercial, and political buildings all encircle the agora. The diagram could lead to a discussion of the highly political nature of Athenian religion and the fact that little distinction was made between sacred and secular space.

Questions to Consider

This section asks students to make fairly sophisticated distinctions among ideals, reality, and idealizations of reality. Once they have divided their lists of personal qualities found in Athenians into these three categories, it would be enlightening to compare lists and have students justify their placement of any qualities about which they disagree. Some students, for example, may choose to take Pericles at his word; others may be more skeptical and critical in their assessments. This is also the time to note conflicting ideals, particularly those conflicts between Plato and everyone else on the issue of ideal female behavior. You may wish to discuss differing views of reality, especially those of the author of Source 4 and Pericles in regard to Athens' treatment of its neighbors and the merits of democracy. Students are also asked to divide their lists of personal qualities according to sex and social status. This task should not pose any problems because the authors of the sources are explicit on this issue. You may wish to point out that Plato is the only one to make distinctions among women on the basis of their abilities; all the others speak of "women" as an undifferentiated category. (In fact, though they simply say "women," they are talking about citizens' wives. Slave women in Athens were not confined to women's quarters because they had to fetch water and do the marketing and laundry. Physically they were freer than citizens' wives, but they suffered double discrimination because of their status both as slaves and as women. Adultery among men was not considered a crime in ancient Athens, and slave women were frequently sexually exploited by their masters.)

The Athenian definition of democracy may also provoke some disagreement among your students. Here the hypothetical definitions of Pericles, Plato, and Socrates might be compared in order to demonstrate the wide variance of opinion among the male citizenry. This would be a good place to explore the way people's opinions about a subject shape the words they choose to define that subject.

Epilogue and Evaluation

The epilogue mentions other types of idealizations in ancient Athens and discusses the effects of Athenian ideals on the later development of Western culture. Using a quotation from Edith Hamilton, it stresses the fact that these idealizations were accepted as close to reality until the twentieth century. Given the status of women in ancient Athens, the fact that this passage was written by a woman is particularly striking. The students are asked to assess Hamilton's judgment, given what they have read in this chapter. You may wish to broaden the discussion with speculations about why a woman would use such terms as *balance*, *harmony*, and *clarity* to describe a culture that was so restrictive of women. (Be sure your students note the sexist nature of her language in this passage.)

The chapter ends with the comment that though many aspects of Athenian culture were emulated by later Western cultures, democratic government would not be attempted again for another two thousand years. At this point it is probably too early in the course for students to speculate on the reasons for this phenomenon, but you may wish to return to the issue later in the course. Why did the Romans, who admired and copied so much of Athenian culture, not attempt direct democracy on the Athenian model? Why was medieval society uniformly hierarchical? (Though there is some speculation that the early Germans possessed a sort of rough-and-ready warrior democracy, this presumed "democracy" preceded the introduction of writing into Germanic society, and we have no sources that directly attest to it. The most vocal advocates of this idea are nationalistic German historians whose judgments are somewhat questionable.) How did the democracies that began to be established in the modern period differ from that of classical Athens, in both ideals and reality?

This chapter lends itself to inventive methods of evaluation. A classroom debate about the merits and nature of Athenian democracy is one possibility. Students could also rewrite Pericles' speech from the perspective of a slave or woman. Their work could be evaluated with a more formal written assignment, of course, and this would be a good opportunity to spot any problems they might have in reading and understanding somewhat complex material.

For Further Reading

Jill N. Claster, ed., *Athenian Democracy: Triumph or Travesty?* (1967). A collection of essays and excerpts on Athenian democracy and imperialism.

A. H. M. Jones, *Athenian Democracy* (1957). A balanced introduction to the subject.

Eva Keuls, *The Reign of the Phallus: Sexual Politics in Ancient Athens* (1985). Using little-known vase paintings as evidence, the author makes a strong case for the extremely misogynist nature of Athenian culture. Includes good discussions of prostitution and homosexuality.

H. D. F. Kitto, *The Greeks* (1951). The classic discussion of all aspects of Athenian life. Wonderfully written and very pro-Athenian.

R. Meiggs, *The Athenian Empire* (1972). Discusses the transformation of the Athenian alliance into an empire and the Peloponnesian War.

Sarah Pomeroy, *Goddesses, Whores, Wives and Slaves: Women in Classical Antiquity* (1975). One of the first and still best discussions of women in the ancient world; examines mythology, artistic evidence, legal sources, and tomb inscriptions.

Charles A. Robinson, *Athens in the Age of Pericles* (1959). A good brief description, with many excerpts from original sources.

William Linn Westermann, "Slavery and the Elements of Freedom in Ancient Greece," *Quarterly Bulletin of the Polish Institute of the Arts and Sciences in America*, January 1943, pp. 1–16. Explores the nature of Greek slavery and the relation between slavery and philosophical ideas.

Thomas Wiedemann, ed., *Greek and Roman Slavery* (1981). A sourcebook with over two hundred selections taken from inscriptions, literature, legal documents, and other sources.

CHAPTER THREE

The Achievements of Augustus

This chapter takes to heart Ralph Waldo Emerson's comment, "There is no history, only biography." Though "great man" history is somewhat out of fashion among professional historians, it is still popular with many students, and Augustus serves as a good example from the ancient world. At first glance, Julius Caesar may appear the more obvious example, but his achievements were primarily military and literary rather than legal and institutional. Because many of us in our race through the course materials choose to focus on law and government when discussing Rome, Augustus is the more appropriate choice of the two. Julius Caesar's assassination also tends to provoke counterfactual questions (What would have happened had Caesar not been assassinated?) that are fascinating as speculation but do not really help students learn how to handle original sources.

Through the sources in this chapter, students will realize that the issue of "greatness" is a double one, involving both real achievements and posterity's judgments about those achievements. They will also see in Augustus an individual who consciously manipulated public opinion to make sure he would later be judged great. His actions should stimulate discussion of the whole issue of "greatness" and help students understand why many historians no longer use the word.

The Problem

Content objectives:

1. to identify the main achievements of Augustus

2. to see how Augustus transformed the Roman Republic into an empire while maintaining the formal apparatus of a republic

3. to understand the power of tradition in Roman culture

4. to distinguish between *de jure* and *de facto* political power

5. to understand how symbols communicated and extended the reputation of Augustus

Skills objectives:

1. to reconcile conflicting opinions about a historical figure

2. to separate process from results when analyzing changes

3. to make judgments about an author's objectivity

4. to make conclusions from evidence presented through maps

On a larger scale, you may wish to use "The Achievements of Augustus" to stimulate discussion on one or more of the following questions:

1. Why did the Roman senate not see what was happening? Or, if it did, why did the senators not resist more strongly the changes Augustus was making? If Rome had been a republic for so long, why was there no popular revolt against Augustus?

2. Do you think Augustus really believed he was simply restoring and reforming the Republic? If not, why wouldn't he take the title of emperor?

3. Other than the fact that they were paid by the emperor, what reasons can you see for the fact that so many writers were attracted to Augustus?

The chapter is also an obvious springboard for a much broader discussion of the relationship between actual political power in any state and the theoretical form of government. To help students understand Augustus's strategies and the reasons for his success, you may wish to introduce sources from a modern state in which actual power and the official form of government have been quite divergent. The Soviet Union and Eastern European countries during the cold war provide one possibility, as do many military regimes in South America. For that matter, testimony during the Iran-Contra hearings in the United States would provide an excellent example of individuals carrying out extralegal actions while claiming to be operating within an established political system.

Sources and Method

The first question in this chapter is the easier of the two but still requires extremely careful reading of the sources, because it asks students not only to identify Augustus's acts but also to see how these deeds transformed the Republic into an empire. If your students are having difficulty with this task, you may wish to make it a two-step process. In the first step, students read and examine the evidence and list all the actions of Augustus mentioned there. (Some of his deeds will, of course, be mentioned in more than one source.) In the second step, students decide which of the actions on their list altered the balance of power in Rome, and how. The chapter points out that Augustus rarely changed the form of government, so you should encourage students to look for situations in which actual power changed hands or in which Augustus asserted his authority behind the scenes. This will require comparative analysis of sources. For example, in Source 1, Augustus plays four different roles in the issuing of this decree. Because the senate has given him direct control of the provinces, he sends the decree out to them on his own authority. He comments that it has been passed by the senate, but close reading indicates he had a hand in that, too. The senators first issued this decree when Augustus asked the consuls to bring the matter before them. At that time he claimed to be acting on the recommendation of a council, but it was one he himself had appointed; and when the senate passed the original decree, Augustus was "one of those present at the writing." Thus what seems at first glance like a simple extension of a senate decree to the provinces emerges instead as a proclamation reflecting the will of Augustus at every stage of the process. Similar examples of manipulation appear in several of the other sources as well.

Your introduction to this chapter will be determined in part by the information students can gain from the textbook you are using. Most texts, and the "Problem" section in this chapter, discuss the structure of Roman government. It is important, however, for students to see how actual power operated within that structure during the period of the late Republic. During the first century B.C., power within the senate had already been concentrated in the hands of a small number of families. The enormous size of the senate (even before Augustus enlarged it further) probably made such a concentration inevitable, but it meant that most senators were already accustomed to supporting the wishes of their leaders. Thus, Augustus's moves are perhaps less dramatic than they seem. The long period of unrest and revolts beginning with the Gracchi revolt of 133 B.C. made Romans more willing—indeed eager—to accept strong leadership.

Social changes since the end of the Punic Wars had also left many Romans nostalgic for what they perceived as the "good old days." The wars had impoverished many farmers, forcing them to sell their land and move to the city of Rome. This land was often purchased by a new class of superrich who flaunted their wealth with elaborate villas, yachts, and racehorses. Not only did Augustus provide money and spectacles for the poor in Rome, but he also forbade conspicuous consumption and extravagant expenditure in the city, reforms that made him very popular with the people, who saw him as returning Rome to its simpler, more egalitarian past. This is perhaps the reason, as Suetonius reports, that "the whole body of citizens with a sudden unanimous impulse proffered him the title of father of his country." (Of course, it is difficult to understand how "the whole body of citizens" could do anything unanimously, given the fact that the number of citizens in Rome alone numbered in the hundreds of thousands. What Suetonius actually meant by this statement is a matter you may wish to discuss.)

The Evidence

Students are using several different types of evidence in this chapter, and you may wish to emphasize the fact that each type must be read somewhat differently. Sources 1 and 2 are decrees, but because we are searching for changes in actual power relationships rather than simply changes in laws, our primary interest in them is not what they actually set down but the way in which they were passed. We have already pointed out the multifaceted role played by Augustus in issuing Source 1. In Source 2 the vow taken in the first paragraph and the reasons given for choosing the date of each sacrifice (for example, "the day on which he first entered upon command of the world") tell us more about the provincial attitude toward Augustus than does the fact that six individuals will be chosen to provide sacrifices, incense, and wine.

   In Sources 3 through 7 students directly confront the issue of objectivity. Horace's piece is, of course, an ode, and as such provides a model of flowery nonobjectivity. (You may wish to compare this ode with its modern equivalent, the introduction of a speaker to his audience, though perhaps only funeral eulogies are as extravagant as this.) In Source 7, Augustus is recording his own actions in what appears to be a straightforward manner; yet this example can illustrate the ways in which word choice can shape a reader's opinion of actions and events, as in the sentence "I liberated the Republic, which was oppressed by the tyranny of a faction." Though the self-serving tone may be what one expects in an autobiography, the care that Augustus takes to show that all his changes were approved by the senate demonstrates that his ego never blinded him to Roman notions of propriety and tradition. He thus appears to be quite objective, but can one ever be in an autobiography? Sources 4 through 6 were written by historians, whom students (and many of us) expect to be somewhat objective. Once these selections have been weighed for their bias and objectivity, you may wish to broaden the discussion in one of several ways. One possibility is to ask whether all cultures have seen objectivity as a virtue in the writing of history. Would Romans have expected their historians to be objective, or wanted them to be? Another issue is whether any historian writing about Augustus could be objective, given the way in which the emperor manipulated public opinion and the public record. Both these topics beg a much larger question, of course: whether it is ever possible to be objective in writing history, given the fact that every historian has biases and the record is always somewhat skewed. Would not making clear one's biases and the limitations of the sources accomplish the same goal more honestly?

In their analyses of the coins and arch, students venture into the world of political symbols, which will be discussed more fully in Chapter 6 of Volume I. (You may, at that point, want to return to this chapter for further examples of symbols of power.) Augustus's adroit manipulation of symbols is an important part of his success in winning power and certainly of his assessment as "great" by posterity.

Students may need some assistance in answering the questions posed about the maps. In his autobiography, Augustus comments that he extended the boundaries of the Empire and restored peace to many areas, especially those in its western half. The Romans built their roads initially for military purposes; one of the best ways to "restore peace" was to make sure that the legions could quickly reach any trouble spots. Thus Augustus concentrated his road building in those parts of the Empire he wanted to pacify. The eastern half of the Empire had older roads built by the Persians or Greeks, so the need for new ones was not as great as in the west. Once the roads were built, of course, they promoted commerce and trade as well as the rapid movement of troops. The U.S. interstate highway system provides a close parallel; this road system, too, was built initially for military purposes but then became a vital commercial network.

Questions to Consider

This section asks students to bring together what they have learned. Because the evidence is so varied, they may need some assistance in figuring out how the pieces fit together. Augustus gained power in many realms—political, military, economic, religious, ideological. It will be useful for students first to separate these areas, then to decide which realm they believe to be most significant, and finally to see how the emperor's increasing power in one realm was tied to that in others. This will help them to answer the second question, about the reasons for Augustus's success, as well as the first. In answering the second question, they should also note the interplay between Augustus's increasing power on one hand and changes and continuities in symbolism on the other. Because he recognized the power of Roman traditions, Augustus did not adopt new symbols but transformed those already used by the Republic. At times his alterations were quite subtle, so you may have to guide students' analyses of the titles, images, and ceremonies.

Because this chapter is somewhat historiographic in its purposes, students are asked to consider whether eyewitness reports or later secondary accounts are more likely to be accurate. This issue can be linked to the earlier discussion of objectivity and also can be opened up into a much broader discussion using contemporary examples. Some historians would assert that "history" cannot be written until at least fifty years after events have occurred. Does the evidence in this chapter support this view? If part of your course is an ongoing dialogue about the nature of history, "The Achievements of Augustus" should contribute to that discussion.

Epilogue and Evaluation

The epilogue returns the issue of Augustus's success to its historical context by providing information on the ways in which future emperors built on his achievements. You may wish to make distinctions between those who continued to respect Roman traditions and are judged "good" emperors, such as Marcus Aurelius, and those who defied tradition and are uniformly regarded as bad, such as Caligula.

This chapter may be evaluated in a number of different ways. You may wish to approach the issue of Augustus's "greatness" directly by setting up a classroom debate between those who regard his achievements as equal to his reputation and those who view the latter as inflated by the emperor's supporters. You may also choose to arrange a debate about a somewhat different question. Though the issue of inevitability is a dangerous one, you may approach it obliquely by framing the debate in terms of a question such as this: "Given the civil war after the death of Julius Caesar, was a strong executive necessary?" If you are teaching the entire Western Civilization course, you could return to this issue when you discuss the career of another "great man," Napoleon. The chapter may also be evaluated through a written assignment centering on the two questions: the first will enable you to see how well your students are comprehending their reading; the second, how well they can develop an argument based on that reading.

For Further Reading

M. Hammond, *The Augustan Principate* (1933). Specifically discusses political and legal developments.

A. H. M. Jones, *Augustus* (1970). The best modern account of the life and times of Augustus and the government he instituted.

F. Millar, *The Emperor in the Roman World* (1977). Discusses the political and ideological role played by Roman emperors from Augustus on.

Victor von Hagen, *The Roads That Led to Rome* (1967). A thorough discussion of all aspects of Roman roads; many photographs and diagrams.

C. M. Wells, *The German Policy of Augustus* (1972). Uses archaeological findings to illustrate Roman expansion into northern Europe.

CHAPTER FOUR

The Development of Orthodoxy
in Early Christianity

The early history of Christianity can be a difficult topic to teach for several reasons. One is the problem of sources. Other than the accounts given in the New Testament, which most biblical scholars date from the last half of the first century A.D., no contemporary records of the life of Jesus survive, making it impossible to verify even his existence through non-Christian written sources. It was hoped that the Dead Sea Scrolls, written by a Jewish group living at roughly the same time as Jesus, might provide specific evidence, but now that they have been largely transcribed it is clear that they do not. Neither can they be used to disprove New Testament accounts, for scholars disagree on their exact dates, with estimates ranging from about 200 B.C. to A.D. 60. Because the books of the New Testament that describe events in Jesus' life were collations of stories and accounts that had circulated orally, they sometimes conflict with one another, making the New Testament even more problematic as a historical source.

The religious commitments of many of our students also make teaching about the early Church difficult. Those who have an intellectual and emotional commitment to Christianity are sometimes unwilling to accept how little is actually certain about their religion's early history. Non-Christians, as well as those who have reacted against Christianity or organized religion in general, may think that an uncertain historical record indicates falsehood. Class discussions can sometimes lapse into polemics, with some students feeling insulted. Basic knowledge of Christian ideas and concepts also varies widely within introductory level classes, for on very few other topics do we find students who have memorized the basic texts. This range of background is becoming more pronounced as non-Western students enroll in Western Civilization classes in greater numbers.

Because of these problems, it might be easier to skip this period of Christian history; indeed, some textbooks on the history of Christianity start with the activities of Paul. Textbooks on U.S. history, especially those designed for high school students, often leave out religion as much as possible to avoid controversy, thereby skewing such stories as the establishment of the New England colonies. We feel, however, that precisely because our students are growing more diverse, it is important for them to understand the beginnings of what would become the most important institution in Europe. It is also important for them to learn how the historical approach differs from that of theologians and philosophers. In his *Decline and Fall of the Roman Empire*, Gibbon offered a rather pessimistic view of this difference: "The theologian may indulge in the pleasing task of describing Religion as She descended from Heaven, arrayed in her native purity. A more melancholy duty is imposed on the historian. He must discover the inevitable mixture of error and corruption which she contracted in a long residence upon Earth, among a weak and degenerate race of beings."

The Problem

Content objectives:

1. to identify and understand some of the central ideas in Christianity

2. to learn about the diversity within early Christianity

3. to understand how standards of authority were first established in early Christianity

4. to see how the content of ideas may be shaped by the process through which they are disseminated, and vice versa

Skills objectives:

1. to read religious sources critically for the historical information they contain

2. to compare different accounts of the same event

3. to recognize differences in theories of historical causation

4. to discuss religious traditions and institutions in the same way that politics and economics are discussed, using differences of opinion constructively

In addition, you may wish to discuss a number of broader questions, including one or more of the following:

1. In terms of its ideas, what made Christianity different from all the other religious options available to first-century Romans, such as traditional Roman religion and other mystery religions like those of Isis and Mithras?

2. Why did early leaders of the Church, such as Irenaeus, feel it imperative to reduce the acceptable interpretations of the message of Jesus? Which of their motivations might have derived from the content of Christian ideas, and which from the Roman social and political setting?

3. Other than the two texts from Nag Hammadi (Sources 3 and 4), all the descriptions of gnostic ideas come from individuals who were hostile to them. What problems does this pose for our interpretation? What special techniques must we as historians use when confronted with hostile texts? What do we do when such texts are our only sources?

4. Do you see any possible problems arising from the fact that orthodox Christianity developed both an authoritative text (the New Testament) and an authoritative body of individuals (the bishops)? (This might be an issue to come back to when you are discussing the Reformation, in which the text was privileged and the individuals were rejected.) How might this duality make Christianity different from other world religions that were not based on a single text (such as many Eastern religions) or did not have individuals who were granted special authority?

Depending on the background and make-up of your class, you may wish to make use of the religious diversity and expertise of your students to broaden the discussion still further. Students who have an intimate knowledge of the New Testament might be asked to supply examples from other parts of the Gospels or other books of the Bible that support or contradict the ideas of both orthodox writers and the gnostics. Jewish students might be asked to assess how the variant views of the nature and purpose of Jesus fit with Jewish concepts of the Messiah. Those who are aware of contemporary differences of opinion within their own or other denominations might be asked to compare these with the differences noted in this chapter. Those who come from religious traditions other than Christianity might be asked to describe parallels within their own traditions. (We have found that the level of familiarity with any religious tradition outside the Judeo-Christian one is extremely low among most U.S. students, and the knowledge they do have is often inaccurate. For this reason, the sharing of even very simple information can be quite useful. This also applies to familiarity with Catholicism among Protestants and to familiarity with many Protestant denominations among students from other backgrounds.)

You may wish to expand the discussion into the nature of human institutions. Can any institution survive without a hierarchy of authority? If students have mentioned other teachings of Jesus in their discussion, such as the Sermon on the Mount (Matthew 5.1–7.7), you might ask them to consider whether any human institution could operate according to the principles these teachings outline.

Sources and Method

The central questions in this chapter require students to read the sources for two kinds of information: information about the content of ideas and information about the process of historical change. Though one of the chapter's purposes is to demonstrate how these are related, it might be useful to suggest that, on first reading, students keep the two kinds of information distinct. Particularly with Sources 1 through 4, they could focus first on the content of Christian ideas and then consider the process of change. (Because these first four sources all relate events that occurred after the crucifixion, you may need to describe Jesus' trial and crucifixion or have one of your students who is well-versed in the New Testament do so.)

The questions in this section directed to the students are quite specific, and it may be useful to ask them to write down their answers in two columns—orthodox and gnostic—so that they can compare the two more easily. The questions revolve primarily around two concepts: the nature of Jesus' resurrection and the nature of the group to whom he gave authority. The most obvious points of comparison for the former are Matthew 24:36–43, in which Jesus demonstrates his physical nature in two different ways, and line seven of "The Wisdom of Jesus Christ," in which he is explicitly described as an invisible spirit. Concerning his disciples, the most obvious points of comparison are the first line of Source 2, which notes only eleven male disciples (those gathered at Galilee), and the first line of Source 4, which indicates that there were twelve men and seven women. Astute students might pick out, however, that even in this gnostic source the men are described as "disciples" and the women simply as "women." You might ask them to think about why this was so, and why this might have made the events described in Source 3 disturbing even to some gnostic Christians. (Again, depending on the background of your class, you may need to provide a brief introduction to the various people discussed in these readings, particularly Peter and Mary Magdalene.)

Sources 5 through 7 will provide further evidence of ways in which orthodox and gnostic interpretations varied, allowing your students to expand their lists. They will also see that the gnostics differed widely from each other. At least according to Irenaeus, Saturninus and Basilides both held that

Jesus was totally spiritual, whereas Cerinthus regarded him as a human on whom the spirit of Christ had descended for a while. The Apostles' Creed addresses both of these positions, stressing both the divine and the human nature of Jesus. It also explicitly links Jesus with the god who created the universe, describing Jesus as the god's son. Source 7 reveals a probable reason why this clause was placed first in the Apostles' Creed, for Marcion and some other gnostics believed that the god who created the universe was evil, making the universe itself evil and the people who had a special relationship with this god, the Jews, tainted. This belief was the source of many gnostics' strong anti-Semitic ideas as well as their hostility to material things and the body.

Marcion's establishment of a gnostic "canon," described in Source 7, is seen by most historians as the direct inspiration for the establishment of an orthodox canon, described in Source 8. With Source 8 we have moved into sources that focus more on process than on content; as your students answer the questions about this source, it might be helpful for you to point out that the author makes no specific mention of the content of ideas, other than to note that Marcion's ideas were rejected. His reasoning for the acceptance or rejection of certain texts is almost completely a matter of process, or what might better be termed traditions and practices (for example, his comment that though certain books such as Timothy and Titus were personal, they "have been hallowed by being held in honour by the Catholic Church"). You may also wish to discuss how the emphasis on the antiquity of acceptable texts, mentioned in reference to the rejection of the *Shepherd of Hermas*, worked against the gnostic idea of secret and continuing revelation.

Sources 9, 10, and 11 discuss the development of the notion of apostolic authority, which becomes the key factor in determining the orthodoxy of any idea or individual. This is a complex development, and you might wish to point out that the links among individuals described by Irenaeus were largely a matter of tradition, though he regarded them as historical. If a number of your students come from Protestant backgrounds, this would be a good place to discuss the fact that all orthodox Christianity before the Protestant Reformation regarded tradition as just as valid as Scripture in determining the importance of many issues within the Church; the same continues to be true in Roman Catholicism and Orthodox Christianity today. Protestant students often have difficulty understanding that to restrict the central ideas of Christianity to those found in the Bible is to apply a standard that no medieval Christian thinker would have accepted. Introducing this notion here might help them understand why Luther's rejection of papal authority, discussed at length in Chapter 13, was so dramatic. It might also help make the larger distinction between arguing about ideas within a certain set of assumptions (as the medieval Scholastics did when they argued with each other) and radically changing those assumptions (as the Protestant Reformation did).

The Evidence

As part of your background to the evidence, you may wish to discuss what biblical scholars now generally accept about the chronology of the books of the New Testament, particularly because the age of the documents becomes such an important issue in determining their inclusion in the orthodox canon. The Gospel of Luke is generally held to have been written around A.D. 70 to 80 by an associate of Paul's, who also may have written the Acts of the Apostles, which some scholars see as essentially a continuation of Luke. Luke builds on material that was included in the Gospel of Mark, which most scholars regard as the first Gospel to have been written, and includes much of the same material as the Gospel of Matthew, which was probably written at about the same time as Luke. These three Gospels, though each takes a slightly different approach, view Jesus in a largely historical way, stressing his fulfillment of Old Testament prophecies and the events of his life; they are often called the "synoptic Gospels," meaning that they have similar perspectives. The Gospel of John, generally regarded as written later than the other three, is completely different, viewing Jesus in a spiritual or theological rather than historical way and stressing Jesus' divinity. John downplays the importance of the twelve Apostles, describing instead the large number of people who followed Jesus. An interesting paper topic, for a student who wishes to delve further into the issue, would be to compare the view of Jesus' purpose and message in the Gospel of John with that of Sources 3 and 4. The comparison might be quite different from the one done for this chapter.

Though there is some disagreement, most scholars think that the two gnostic texts contained in this chapter date from some time in the second century, after the age of the Apostles. For these sources, and also for Irenaeus's description of gnostic beliefs, your students may need assistance in deciphering mystical notions such as the ascent of the soul or the generation of the 365 heavens. Although such texts may be difficult, the mysticism they express is such a significant part of Western religious tradition that we feel it is worth the trouble of slogging through them. The complexity of the mystical ideas may help demonstrate that gnosticism was only for an intellectual elite, although you may wish to come back to this issue when discussing the concept of popular piety in Chapter 10; by the late Middle Ages mysticism had become a part of the religious experience of a broad range of the population, including the uneducated.

Questions to Consider

This section asks students to be more speculative about why certain ideas became key parts of orthodoxy. The matter is best addressed in conjunction with your textbook's account of Roman society. One of the central trends identified by many scholars of the early Church was a desire to make the Church more acceptable to Roman authorities by reducing its appearance of revolutionary egalitarianism. This meant de-emphasizing the role played by members of normally dependent social groups such as slaves or women and stressing the role of authorities in maintaining order. Another trend, however, which in some ways contradicts the first, was the desire to take in as many people as possible, to make the Church, in the words of an early orthodox leader, a "school for sinners rather than a company of saints."

Though in theory gnostics taught that anyone could have an equally valid vision of Christ, in practice their ideas were spread only to a small group, to those whom other gnostics regarded, in the words of "The Wisdom of Jesus Christ," as "worthy of knowledge." Thus gnosticism became more elitist than orthodoxy. The strong emphasis on secrecy and the importance of oral communication as opposed to written also limited the spread of gnostic ideas; as Church historians and theorists of language such as Walter Ong have pointed out, orthodox Christianity began to spread at just the time that Western culture was changing from a predominantly oral culture to a predominantly manuscript one. Orthodox Christianity made use of the strengths of both types of communication, in the same way that Protestant Christianity, developing at another point of change in the basic medium of communication, drew on both manuscript and print, as we will see in Chapter 13.

The final questions in this section ask students to think about ideas of causation and changing views of the actions of God in history. The purpose of these questions is not to make early Christians seem gullible or superstitious, but to show how easily they blended notions of human and divine causation. Even students who accept the working of God in history tend to posit divine intervention as a cause only when human explanations are insufficient, whereas people like Irenaeus (and many of the authors in Chapters 10 and 13) often saw human decisions and actions as signs of God's choosing to work through human agents.

Epilogue and Evaluation

The epilogue stresses that the development of orthodoxy has been a long process and is still going on today, and that there is a distinction between heresy and heterodoxy. This latter point is often confusing, and you might wish to make sure students understand the difference. Examples of tolerated heterodoxy within an orthodox institution, such as the charismatic movement within Catholicism in which people speak in tongues, can be compared with a different approach that has been rejected, such as the maintenance of the Latin Mass in some areas. Besides providing a modern example of the distinction between heterodoxy and heresy, this example points to the contemporary power of one of the key ideas in this chapter, apostolic authority. Although some advocates of the Latin Mass have defied the rules of bishops, charismatics have not.

In terms of evaluation, this is not the chapter with which to encourage a formal in-class debate, but it lends itself nicely to research papers that build on the topics discussed here. Students might wish to investigate other "heresies" in early or medieval Christianity, to see how the standards developed in response to the gnostics were later applied. They may wish to investigate other groups influenced by the gnostics, such as the Albigensians. Using this book alone, a paper might compare the ideas of the gnostics with those of the Waldensians and Lollards described in Sources 6 and 7 of Chapter 10. For those of you who teach in denominational colleges, it might be interesting for your students to find examples of the determination of orthodoxy within non-Catholic groups; at times Protestant students see this process as unique to Catholicism. To take this issue beyond a religious context, you might assign research papers using examples of orthodoxy and heresy from political or secular ideological groups.

For Further Reading

David Christie-Murray, *A History of Heresy* (1976). Traces ideas regarded as heresies within Christianity from gnosticism to modern groups such as the Jehovah's Witnesses and various messianic cults.

John Dart, *The Laughing Savior: The Discovery and Significance of the Nag Hammadi Gnostic Library* (1976). A popular account of the Nag Hammadi discovery and debates among scholars about the origins and meaning of gnostic texts.

Jacques Lacarriere, *The Gnostics* (1977). A meditation on and sympathetic discussion of the gnostics of Egypt. Originally in French.

Hyam Maccoby, *Paul and Hellenism* (1991). Traces links between Paul and gnosticism, viewing gnostic anti-Semitism as the source of Christian anti-Semitism. Extremely controversial.

Elaine Pagels, *The Gnostic Gospels* (1980). The best introduction to the Nag Hammadi texts, written for a popular audience.

Andrew Welburn, *The Beginnings of Christianity: Essene Mystery, Gnostic Revelation and the Christian Vision* (1991). Views Christianity, including that of the orthodox New Testament, as closely linked to gnosticism and other esoteric teachings.

CHAPTER FIVE

The Domesday Book and Medieval Statistics

This chapter is unique in two ways. First, it is the only chapter in Volume I that relies totally on a single source. In every other chapter, students are asked to bring together information gained from a variety of sources; here they are asked to dig deeply into one. Some teachers may feel that this approach overemphasizes the importance of Domesday, which certainly does not tell the whole story of medieval rural life. Nevertheless, we think it is important for students to see just how much can be extracted from a single source and how a very familiar source can yield quite new information when one asks new questions of it.

Second, the chapter is the only quantitative one in Volume I. Statistical techniques are a significant feature of contemporary historical analysis, and we could have used them in several other chapters as well. Chapter 8 on the Commercial Revolution, Chapter 9 on the craft guilds, and even Chapter 13 on the spread of the Protestant Reformation could well have included a statistical component. By devoting one whole chapter primarily to quantitative techniques, however, we allow students not only to use statistics but also to think about how statistics are gathered and why certain information is regarded as important. They are drawing conclusions based on statistical evidence and, at the same time, actually performing the calculations. All of this helps demystify quantitative methodology so that students learn to regard it neither as totally objective and authoritative nor as a technique available only to mathematical geniuses.

The Problem

Content objectives:

1. to understand the nature of the Domesday survey

2. to learn about medieval agricultural practices

3. to learn about the social and economic structure of the medieval village

4. to learn what factors promoted economic well-being in the medieval countryside

5. to understand how the values of survey takers affect the form of a survey

Skills objectives:

1. to make basic statistical calculations

2. to draw conclusions from those calculations that interpret what the numbers mean

3. to compare several sets of statistics and draw conclusions based on those comparisons

4. to see how several factors could operate together to shape a statistical pattern

Sources and Method

This chapter requires two introductions, one for content and the other for methodology. In terms of content, we usually discuss the effects of the Norman invasion in some detail, particularly William's highly successful attempts at introducing the Norman pattern of feudalism into England. There is a debate among medieval historians about whether feudalism existed in England before the Norman Conquest, or at least whether the Anglo-Saxon system of reciprocal rights and obligations should be termed "feudalism" even though it often did not involve a fief. Because feudalism itself is a sufficiently complex notion in introductory Western Civilization courses, we do not bring up this debate. No one disputes the fact that William did grant land to his nobles—land that in many cases he had taken from Anglo-Saxon nobles—so the Norman system is clearly feudalism in its classic form. This transfer of land was assisted by the Domesday survey, of course.

Working from the Domesday descriptions reprinted in this chapter, you may wish to draw up a diagram of a typical medieval manor. Your diagram could indicate certain features not evident from the Domesday descriptions, such as the three-field system of rotation, strip plowing, and the lack of fences. The typical English plow team was large (eight oxen) because the soil in much of England was so heavy and full of clay; in others parts of Europe, and those parts of England with lighter soil, the ox teams were smaller. Other environmental factors you may want to mention include: excessive cool, rainy weather, more often a problem for English peasants than heat and drought; summer rains, which often made roads totally impassable, lending even more importance to a mill located in one's own village; and the lack of artificial fertilizers, which meant that oxen provided not only draft power but also the best form of fertilizer to slow down soil deterioration.

Your methodological introduction will depend on the statistical and mathematical expertise your students already possess. Assuming that some students might be insulted if we explained very basic principles, we have not discussed the notions of percentage or average; but for students who lack a mathematical background, you may have to explain these concepts. It is also important to ensure that students understand the meaning of each calculation they are making on the worksheet and why we are asking them to perform that calculation. Population density and average manor size should not be a problem, but you may need to explain the reasoning behind some of the other calculations. For example, by knowing the number of plow teams per square mile, we can figure out how much of the land was being plowed. By knowing the population per plow team, we can get a rough idea of soil fertility. The higher the population per team, the higher the soil fertility and, generally, the higher the population density possible in a county. Thus the figures for population density and population per plow team roughly parallel each other. Yorkshire, with an even lower population density than one would suspect from the population per plow team, is a somewhat anomalous case. This is because villages in Yorkshire were very small and widely scattered on tiny pockets of more fertile soil; more people could be supported per plow team in these pockets than in, say, Shropshire, but the land in between was not arable.

The final four columns of the worksheet are all based on William's surveyors' estimates of how many plow teams a county could theoretically support. Unlike the first six columns, they involve subjective judgments and so must be used carefully. William's surveyors may have inflated the figures because they knew he wanted to sell off the land at high prices, or the local people on whom the surveyors relied for these estimates may have deflated them to indicate to the king that they were using the land as effectively as they could. We could not conscientiously use these figures to compare land use at this time with that at another point in English history, but we can use them as we do here to compare counties at the time of Domesday, for there is no reason to assume that the surveyors would have inflated the figures for one county and deflated them for another. If bias exists, it most probably operates in the same direction in all five counties.

The Evidence

The chapter asks students to answer two questions, one that generalizes about rural society in eleventh-century England and one that makes comparisons among counties. The first question should be relatively easy if students follow the questions in the chapter, but the second requires skill at basing conclusions on statistics; here they may need more assistance. Their comparisons are based both on the tables provided and on the worksheet they have filled in. To facilitate instruction, the worksheet, including the figures, is reproduced on page 36.

Again, the questions should guide students in their conclusions. As we would expect, the figures for population density, average manor size, and plow teams per square mile all parallel one another, with Norfolk scoring the highest in each category and Yorkshire the lowest; we might conclude, then, that soil fertility is highest in Norfolk and lowest in Yorkshire. Looking at Table 5, however, we find that Wiltshire is the most productive county in terms of annual value per square mile, per man, and per plow team. Do these figures indicate that Yorkshire is perhaps too densely populated? That Wiltshire is actually the most fertile? The answer to the latter question is most likely yes, given the fact that the annual value per adult male and plow team is so much higher for Wiltshire than for any other county. More people and more teams worked each square mile in Norfolk, but they produced less. William's surveyors recognized the unusual productivity of Wiltshire in their judgment that the county was producing 86 percent of what it possibly could, a much higher figure than that for the other counties. The extremely low annual values for Yorkshire reinforce the conclusion that the soil there was the least fertile. William's surveyors agreed, judging Yorkshire the lowest in theoretical annual value per square mile. Because Yorkshire could never support the population density of any of the other counties, dramatically increasing Yorkshire's population would not significantly increase the annual value.

WORKSHEET

County	Unadjusted Total Rural Population	Total Rural Population Adjusted for Slaves	Population Density	Average Manor Size	Population per Plow Team	Plow Teams per Sq Mi	Percent of Theoretical Capacity Currently Producing	Highest Theoretical Annual Value	Highest Theoretical Annual Value per Sq Mi	Highest Theoretical Annual Value per Adult Male
Cornwall	24,156	20,096	15	61	16	0.9	48	1,396	21	6.3
Norfolk	118,390	114,985	56	158	23	2.5	—	—	—	—
Shropshire	21,407	18,159	13	40	9	1.5	62	1,374	27	8.3
Wiltshire	44,748	39,190	28	114	13	2.2	86	5,198	80	12.8
Yorkshire	34,047	34,047	5	17	12	0.4	51	2,125	5.9	5.9

The dearth of mills certainly played a role in Cornwall's low level of economic development, as did the large number of mills in Wiltshire's high level. One can easily imagine William's surveyors advising him to encourage the building of mills in counties like Cornwall. They may also have made this suggestion for Yorkshire, because its large size meant that people had to transport their grain great distances to have it ground into flour. Mills are crucial because the medieval diet was predominantly comprised of cereal; unlike the multicourse medieval banquets reenacted today, a typical meal of the Middle Ages would consist of pea soup and dark bread. For people living in Yorkshire, far from a mill and with a growing season too short for wheat, a typical meal would be oatmeal porridge with a few vegetables mixed in, or just oatmeal in the winter. The monotony of such a diet explains why spices were highly prized by all who could afford them and native herbs by those who could not.

Given modern egalitarian ideals, we would hope that social structure had some effect on the economic well-being of these counties. Comparing Tables 5 and 8 indicates that this was not the case, however. Yorkshire had no slaves, but it was still the poorest county. Wiltshire, the most prosperous county in terms of annual value, had no free peasantry, and the majority of its population were slaves or smallholders. Norfolk had the largest percentage of free peasants, but they could not produce as much as the slaves and smallholders of Wiltshire. Clearly, environmental factors such as soil fertility and climate were more significant than social factors in determining how much a county could produce. Not until the seventeenth century, when some rural residents were not only free but in command of enough financial resources and agricultural knowledge to improve the land through fertilization or drainage, would the social structure of the countryside begin to be an important factor in determining agricultural output.

Questions to Consider

This section first asks students to consider the limitations of quantitative analysis, both in general and in terms of the conclusions they have reached for this chapter. In your discussion, you may wish to emphasize the fact that the Domesday surveyors examined rural society from the top down, describing and enumerating only those areas that William was interested in knowing about. The survey gives us no information, for example, about the relations among villagers or about most aspects of daily life. For these matters we must turn to other sources, particularly the manorial court rolls, which provide information about peasant land transfers, inheritance patterns, criminal activity, family and kinship relations, and personal interactions. One way you might expand this chapter, in fact, is to ask students to use the library to discover what other original sources are available for eleventh-century England.

Another problem with the Domesday survey is that the preconceived assumptions of William's surveyors shaped their results. (This is true, of course, in any census.) We know, for example, that a good share of the households in any village were headed by women, usually widows but sometimes unmarried women. Thus the surveyors' count of the total adult male population is not the same as a count of all the households, though in many ways they assumed that it was, and generations of historians since then (including us in this chapter) have used the figure in this way. In arriving at a figure for total rural population, we were able to adjust for slaves because William's surveyors specified the number of adult male slaves in each village; but there is no way to know the exact number of female-headed households, or whether this number varied from county to county, because women were never counted separately. In part this omission came about because William was interested primarily in the number of adult men who could drive ox teams, but it was also the result of medieval attitudes about women. When women were counted or enumerated in any medieval survey, it was usually by marital status, and thus they were defined by their relation to men. The number and status of rural women is only one of many characteristics that the Domesday Book does not address and that we can never know. It may be instructive at this point, particularly if your students have explored other sources available for this period, to have them consider other aspects of rural life we will never know about. Are there features of contemporary culture that historians a thousand years from now will never be able to fathom? Can we even predict what they will be interested in? (This latter question is suggested, of course, by our current interest in women and the family, a topic that would have mystified William's surveyors.)

In expanding the conclusions of the chapter, you may wish to discuss any of the questions suggested in this section, which generally grow out of the way in which the survey was structured and conducted. If you prefer instead to expand on the quantitative material and on students' comparative conclusions, you can have them estimate the missing figures for Norfolk on the worksheet. With its high population density and high population per plow team, the county probably was working very close to its theoretical capacity, for it is hard to imagine many plowlands that were not already being farmed. It was probably not even possible, with such a high population density, for Norfolk to achieve the same annual value per adult male as Cornwall or Yorkshire because there was simply not enough good land. Such estimates are very tentative, of course, but this exercise enables students to see that statistical patterns can be used by historians to make inferences about the past in the same way that economists, sociologists, and political scientists make predictions about the future.

Epilogue and Evaluation

The epilogue discusses both the effects of the Domesday survey and the further history of the document itself. We ask students to recognize that Domesday is an artifact from the eleventh century with its own history as well as simply a source of information. Thus the survey must be physically preserved like any museum object, but its content must also be translated to allow people to use it. In its day, the Domesday survey represented the pinnacle of quantitative record keeping. That peak is being achieved again in our own day through the Santa Barbara/Hull project, which will computerize the entire text.

The way in which you evaluate this chapter will depend partly on how much assistance you want to give students in performing the actual statistical calculations. Students should be able to fill in the worksheet on their own; the main task in this chapter, after all, is not simply arriving at numbers, but drawing meaningful conclusions from those numbers through logical inference. You can assess students' skills at inference collectively through class discussion or individually by having them write a brief essay prior to class discussion.

For Further Reading

H. S. Bennett, *Life on the English Manor* (1967). The classic study of medieval English rural life. Focuses on the thirteenth century, but many of its conclusions also apply to an earlier period.

Judith Bennett, *Women in the Medieval English Countryside: Gender and Household in Brigstock Before the Plague* (1987). A case study of family relations and women's roles in one medieval village. Based on manorial court rolls, with a thorough discussion of the sources.

Elizabeth Hallam, *Domesday Book Through the Centuries* (1986). A thorough examination of the way in which the Domesday survey has been viewed and utilized since it was recorded. Nicely illustrated.

H. Pirenne, *Economic and Social History of Medieval Europe* (1956). The best general introduction, by a premier medievalist.

Peter Sawyer, *Domesday Book: A Reassessment* (1985). A collection of articles discussing the newest areas of Domesday research, including the Santa Barbara/Hull computerization project.

Doris Mary Stenton, *English Society in the Early Middle Ages* (1951). A brief introduction to all aspects of life in England during this period.

CHAPTER SIX

The Growth of Feudal Monarchy

The subject of feudalism offers a wide range of focuses that we could have chosen for this chapter, but the growth of feudal monarchy in the High Middle Ages seemed especially useful because it ties in well with the political developments covered in other chapters (Chapters 2 and 14, in particular). Rather than concentrate completely on actual political changes, however, we have also provided sources through which students can interpret the role of symbols in expressing and shaping power relationships. Many college students already have some familiarity with feudal ceremonies through historical novels and films or such organizations as the Society for Creative Anachronism; but these sources lead them to conceive the Middle Ages as a fairy-tale world of lords, knights, and castles. Rather than simply ignoring those romanticized notions, this chapter places them in a social and political context and allows students to see the ways in which ceremonies, crowns, and castles interwove with royal actions to bring about and express political change.

In writing this chapter, we have used theories of the role of symbolism that were first developed not by historians but by cultural anthropologists and literary critics. Semiotics is an exploding field at the moment, and one that provokes a good deal of controversy, particularly when it is combined with the deconstructive analysis of language. Much of the debate surrounding these schools of thought is esoteric, involving terminology that is both unfamiliar and itself a point of dispute. Thus we have avoided the technical terminology of semiotics in our questions about symbolism in this chapter, but have nonetheless tried to convey some of its basic points, such as the reciprocal relationship between a symbol and what it stands for and the multilayered nature of much symbolism. By asking students to interpret the symbolic meaning of events or objects simultaneously with the actual effects of specific actions, we hope to guard against the anachronism or ahistoricity that can sometimes be a problem in semiotic analysis.

The Problem

Content objectives:

1. to understand the nature of feudalism as a system of rights and obligations

2. to learn how feudal monarchies developed

3. to learn how medieval monarchs expressed their authority

4. to examine some facets of the relationship between Church and state in the Middle Ages

Skills objectives:

1. to examine visual evidence for its political and symbolic content

2. to assess power relationships from proclamations, chronicles, and descriptions of ceremonies

3. to judge the impact a ceremony might have on both participants and observers

4. to learn how to distinguish symbols of authority from the real source of that authority, and to describe how the two are related

You may wish to broaden the discussion further in a number of ways. One would be to expand the discussion of political symbolism chronologically, examining the use of symbolism in earlier cultures (Augustus was very skillful at this kind of display, as the evidence in Chapter 3 makes clear) or in later cultures up to the present. You may also want to talk about the social history of symbolism, the way in which different groups in a society use and interpret symbols. Though all of the evidence about symbols in this chapter refers to their use by figures of authority, you may wish to introduce other sources that portray how peasants or workers expressed themselves symbolically. The flag with the *Bundschuh,* the bound shoe worn by poor people that served as an emblem in the 1525 German peasants' revolt, would provide a good counterpart to the crowns and scepters depicted here, and would link this chapter with the visual and verbal portrayals of different population groups in Reformation propaganda (Chapter 13).

Another possibility, which would take the discussion out of the realm of symbols, is to expand on the idea, introduced in the Sources and Method section, that political history is the study of power rather than politics. How can the two be distinguished in a past society? In our own? Along with traditional political sources, what other sources would one use to study power as distinct from politics? In which societies have the official political system and the actual operation of power been closely linked? In which societies have they been quite separate? (Again, Augustus provides one example of the latter.) What sorts of power relationships existed in medieval society that were unrelated to politics? In our own society?

This last comparison may be used to introduce a more general discussion of the relationship between the family and the political system, as well as the personal rather than institutional nature of medieval political relationships. You may wish to explore continuities as well as contrasts, encouraging your students to consider the political nature of modern family relationships. Because this chapter asks them to broaden their notion of "political," you may find it appropriate to mention the feminist view that "the personal is political," a view that fits medieval feudalism very well. We have found that applying this concept to an analysis of modern power relationships often provokes vigorous debate, no matter what the political opinions of the students or the instructor. It may even serve as a spark for those who claim they have no political opinions.

Sources and Method

Because the chapter and most probably the textbook you are using discuss feudalism in some detail, you may not need to provide much specific introduction to the content of this chapter. You may find that students are still somewhat confused, however, because feudalism appears to be a rather chaotic system of government, with no clear notion of land ownership or sharp distinctions between the kingship and the king. In many ways, feudalism, even in its monarchical version, was indeed chaotic and confusing, so it is important not to make the system appear too orderly. Modern government is only slightly more rationally organized, of course, a fact that you may impress on your students by asking them to consider how many different governmental units they live within and how many governmental agencies have jurisdiction over them or their property. City, county, state, and nation are only the beginning; many areas are also divided among sewer and water districts, school districts, airport commissions, court districts, multicounty or multistate planning boards, community college districts, and metropolitan planning boards. All of these divisions are supported by taxation, and all can compel citizens to comply with their decisions. Even land ownership is not a clear-cut principle, because mineral, water, and even air rights do not always accompany the sale of a piece of property, and government at many levels can confiscate land whenever it wishes through the right of eminent domain. Subinfeudation is still with us, though in a modified form. These modern parallels may help your students comprehend more fully the divided nature of authority in feudalism and appreciate the barriers to the establishment of royal power faced by monarchs such as William the Conqueror and Frederick Barbarossa.

As you make sure your students understand the layers of power and authority in feudalism, you also need to encourage them to realize that those layers were always changing. Subinfeudation occurred constantly, and fiefs were transferred from family to family through marriage or contractual agreements. Different layers asserted their power at different times. Here, again, a more familiar situation might provide a useful comparison, for the buildup of royal power parallels in some ways the changes in the form of the U.S. government from the Articles of Confederation to the Constitution. Authority was far more decentralized under the Articles than under the Constitution, with the states unwilling to grant the national government much actual power; in the same way, feudal vassals asserted their independent legal, economic, and military rights in the First Feudal Age and fought the centralizing moves traced in the sources for this chapter. Under the Constitution the national government, like feudal monarchies, became much stronger, but the states still exist as separate entities that retain some specific powers; similarly, medieval monarchs did not completely do away with the power of the vassals.

Modern parallels may also offer assistance in introducing the issue of political symbols, but there is a danger here. Because most students are extremely experienced television viewers, exposed since early childhood to multimedia events and audience manipulation, it might be hard to convince them that medieval coronation ceremonies were anything more than a monarch's attempt to impress his vassals. Precisely because so much of modern politics, in an era of photo opportunities and sound bites, is strictly symbolic, it may be difficult for your students to imagine a time when people were not somewhat cynical about the use of political symbols. They may find it hard to accept that the monarch or his subjects might have sincerely believed in the ideas a coronation ceremony was meant to embody. Thus, in the sources that describe actual legal maneuvers by monarchs as well as symbolic actions, you may need to help students more in identifying the former than the latter.

Another problem students may have is understanding why ceremonies were regarded as so extraordinary. One of the characteristics of the premodern world that is hardest for them to grasp is the relative lack of visual stimulation in most people's lives. Other than flowers in bloom, the medieval world was largely gray, green, and brown; the lack of artificial dyes and the expense of many natural ones meant that clothing and household linens were usually not dyed (though they may have been bleached). The interiors and exteriors of houses were also shades of brown. Thus a tournament or a ceremony like those described in this chapter would have been impressive simply because of the colors worn by the wealthy noble participants. Buildings could also be impressive by virtue of sheer size; to a person whose village was made up of two-room houses and a one-room church, a castle or cathedral was a stunning sight.

The Evidence

The central task in this chapter involves a two-step process. The first is to analyze three somewhat distinct types of actions on the part of feudal monarchs: those that increased royal authority; those that decreased the power of the Church or the vassals; and those that expressed these new power relationships symbolically. The second step is to see how these types of actions were interrelated so that certain royal decisions could accomplish all three aims at once.

Source 1 is a standard chronicle description of William's actions, though it is quite hostile to those actions and to Normans in general. It was chosen primarily because it describes not only military maneuvers, but also William's decisions about building castles and staffing existing fortresses; thus it sets up the visual depictions of castles in Sources 2 through 4. From this text and the pictures, students should easily grasp both the symbolic and the strategic value of castles, though a few points might slip by them. Castle moats and towers had a strategic as well as a symbolic function, for they lent castles a greater sense of height and hence formidability and made it more difficult for archers to shoot over the walls or for soldiers to scale them. (Unless a castle stood on a river bank, the moat was dry, not filled with water as Hollywood depicts. In fact, during times of peace, the moat was often used as a garden and a place to stable animals.) The placement of William's castles reflects his two major military concerns: the possibility of an invasion from the Continent and the unruliness of the Welsh tribes, led, as Orderic notes, by King Blethyn. Though William built castles throughout England, he built them especially along the south coast and the Welsh border.

Sources 5 through 7 are quite straightforward in their descriptions of royal actions and decisions that limited the independent power of the vassals and Church officials. You will want to make sure your students pick up both the assertion of the king's legal power in cases involving the vassals or higher Church officials and the limitation of these individuals' powers over others. The last part of Source 8 provides direct evidence of the investiture controversy, with Pope Hadrian claiming that Frederick Barbarossa had received his imperial crown—and hence, implicitly, his right to rule—from the pope, and Frederick answering that he had received his right to rule from God alone. This is one of the first examples of the argument for what would later be called the divine right of kings, a point brought up in the Questions to

Consider section. It also provides an explicit example of how a fight over investiture (that is, the handing on of symbols of office such as a crown) stood for a dispute over actual sovereignty.

Interpreting the royal portraits should not pose a problem because all clearly portray rulers with both religious and secular symbols of power. Both the portrait of Otto III and the section of the Bayeux Tapestry show the rulers above but surrounded by their nobles and Church officials, thus representing the older notion of kingship in which the king was simply the greatest of the nobles. These stand in sharp contrast to later portraits of such absolutist monarchs as Louis XIV (or of those who wanted to be absolutist, like Charles I), in which the nobles never appear.

In the descriptions of ceremonies, as in the portraits, even the smallest detail may have symbolic value and thus may be seen as affirming power relationships. For example, the author of Source 8 considers it extremely auspicious that Emperor Frederick was crowned on the same day and in the same place that the Bishop of Münster was consecrated. The fact that both men were named Frederick appears to the author to be even greater proof of God's approval of both and a blessing to the links between Church and state.

Questions to Consider

This section asks students to consider the changing power relationships of feudalism more carefully, and to note differences between England and Germany. In terms of the latter point, the most important difference is that the Holy Roman emperorship was an elected position, giving the nobles in the Empire much greater power than those in England. It may be more difficult for your students to understand the relationship between the ruler and the Church than that between the ruler and the vassals, because the medieval Church was so different in form and function from any religious institution with which they are familiar. It is important to stress that a Church official could be both a lord and, often simultaneously, a vassal, swearing fealty to an overlord and claiming homage from lesser nobles. Church officials usually did not perform the military part of their obligations themselves but sent other men as knights, although this was not always the case. In one famous incident, an English bishop determined that it would be acceptable for him to fight as long as he used a mace instead of a sword. He agreed with the generally held notion that it was improper for a man of God to shed blood, but he also reasoned that by using a mace to crush skulls he could kill people without much bloodshed.

The combination of feudal loyalties and religious sentiment this chapter demonstrates can serve as a good introduction to a discussion of the Crusades. More than any other undertaking, the Crusades reflected and resulted from all the qualities that typified the Middle Ages: religious devotion, a sense of honor, personal loyalty to one's superior, a view of Christendom as a fief, a penchant for violence, suspicion of the unfamiliar, and greed for luxuries. Many of these qualities are amply demonstrated in the sources in this chapter.

Epilogue and Evaluation

The epilogue sets into historical context the changes initiated by feudal monarchs. It does so by providing the end of the story, that is, the further transformation of feudal principalities into centralized nation-states. At this point you may wish to emphasize that the Middle Ages mark the last time in history when generalizations about political developments can be made for all of Europe. From 1500 to the present, political history in western Europe will be the story of nation-states; in central Europe, of city-states and fragmented empires. This may also be a good place to point out that nations are not natural or ahistorical but distinct political units that emerged at a certain time in history and thus may disappear again, although recent debates about European unity point out the continuing allegiance to national units. Students often have difficulty imagining a world without nations or nationalism. In the High Middle Ages, of course, the only sentiment akin to nationalism was loyalty to Christendom.

You may wish to emphasize the link suggested in the epilogue between feudalism and later developments by skipping ahead to at least the visual evidence on absolutism in Chapter 14; or you may choose to wait until that part of the course to have students review this chapter for the seeds of absolutist ideas. The last sentence of Source 8 is probably the clearest example, for the author calls Frederick the "anointed of Christ." This passage would also help illustrate the much-diminished role of the Church in later absolutism, for the author also calls the Bishop of Münster "the anointed of Christ," something no seventeenth-century author would do.

This chapter provides a good opportunity for students to undertake a comparative project. This could involve additional research—comparing, for example, the symbols of feudal monarchy with those of the Roman emperorship, the papacy, early modern absolutist monarchs, or a contemporary government. In the last case, it might be interesting to bring in some contemporary states, such as England, that have retained many medieval symbols, and others, such as the United States, whose symbols were originally developed as a rejection of monarchy. The coronation of Queen Elizabeth II is available on videotape and might be fun to compare with that of Richard the Lionhearted. Another possibility for further research would be to explore the use of medieval symbols by later, very different governments. The most obvious example is the Nazis' use of the imperial eagle, supporting their notion of the Third Reich as a reincarnation of the Holy Roman Empire. The Nazis were the absolute masters of ceremonial symbolism, and you might even choose to show *Triumph of the Will* or a similar documentary as a twentieth-century counterpart to the ceremonies your students have read about in this chapter. If you prefer projects that stay within the Middle Ages, students could compare the development of feudal monarchy in two or more countries or examine the comparative importance of symbols in centralized courts, law codes, and nonfeudal armies, showing in each case how the symbols affected the monarchs' assertion of power.

For Further Reading

Marc Bloch, *Feudal Society*, trans L. A. Manyon (1961). Still the best introduction to feudalism, by a great French medievalist. Also provides an introduction to the Annales school's historical perspective.

Robin Frame, *The Political Development of the British Isles* (1990). Traces the expansion of royal government with particular attention to differences within Britain, especially in Wales, Scotland, and Ireland.

Jacques Le Goff, "The Symbolic Ritual of Vassalage," in *Time, Work and Culture in the Middle Ages*, trans. Arthur Goldhammer (1982). Incorporates many ideas from anthropology and semiotics.

Sidney Painter, *The Rise of Feudal Monarchies* (1951). Discusses the theory and practice of feudal monarchy.

Charles Petit-Dutailles, *The Feudal Monarchy in France and England from the 10th to the 13th Century* (1936). A classic comparison, recently reissued.

CHAPTER SEVEN
Life at a Medieval University

Most of what students encounter in the first semester of Western Civilization seems foreign and exotic to them. Though they can identify links and continuities when studying U.S. or even modern European history, they can often see no connection between the premodern world and the contemporary one. You may choose to point out parallels between premodern and modern institutions and events, but these will remain parallels rather than direct connections. To mitigate this sense of total disjunction between the distant past and the present, we have chosen in this chapter to focus on one institution that does have a continuous history from the Middle Ages to the present—the university. This is thus the only chapter in Volume I that explicitly asks students to make comparisons between a historical situation and a contemporary one.

The content of these comparisons (that is, the "answer" to the second question posed in the chapter) will depend on what sort of college or university your students are attending, not simply on their reading of the documents. We have tried to frame the comparative questions so that they are applicable to all forms of modern U.S. higher education; but if some questions are less pertinent to your setting, you may wish to bring out other points of comparison and contrast.

The Problem

Content objectives:

1. to learn how medieval universities and colleges were established and organized

2. to learn why universities were a focus of concern for both Church and state authorities during the Middle Ages

3. to examine medieval student life, both academic and nonacademic

49

4. to understand the similarities and differences between medieval and modern universities

Skills objectives:

1. to write a description based on evidence and then alter this description when new material is presented

2. to assess how an author's identity and intent shapes his or her view of events

3. to weigh the validity of conflicting views of the same institution

4. to assess the logical reasoning in a philosophical argument

As with other chapters, "Life at a Medieval University" may also be used to stimulate discussion about larger questions:

1. What significance is there in the fact that all university education was in Latin, which by the twelfth century was no one's native language? Latin brought both benefits and problems, of course. On the one hand, because Latin was an international language, students could attend any university they chose without encountering a language barrier. This meant that most universities drew students from many different countries, and students could change schools easily. On the other hand, only those with a knowledge of Latin could attend a university. The general liberal arts curriculum of the first several years at the university could help students improve their Latin skills, but they had to know the basics before enrolling. Thus young men from urban areas had a better chance of attending the university than those from small villages, and those from wealthier families a better opportunity than peasants and workers. In addition, because Latin became so closely identified with university study or a career in the Church, activities that were both closed to women, the latter were rarely taught Latin. The noted scholar of language and literature Walter Ong has, in fact, called Latin a male puberty rite, because it served the same functions of peer-group bonding and exclusion of noninitiates that rites such as scarring and adolescent circumcision did in other cultures. Further, a knowledge of Latin was necessary to read most of what was written and copied in the Middle Ages. Women's lack of Latin meant they were unable to read most serious works on their own. (This omission in their education had its positive side, however. Many, and perhaps most, of the translations of literary and religious works in circulation before 1500 were written with female patronage or with women readers in mind.) As part of the discussion,

you may have to point out that at Oxford and Cambridge Latin continued to be the language of instruction in some fields, such as history, until less than one hundred years ago.

2. Were (and are) universities ever the free associations of students and teachers they were envisioned to be? Should state and Church authorities become involved in choosing what is taught at a university? Issues of academic freedom still make headlines, and the sources in this chapter will help students become aware of the long history of attempts to regulate the content of classroom teaching and to restrict the reading of some books and authors. This topic may be used as a transition to a more general question about censorship:

3. Should some ideas and opinions be censored? This is, of course, a very broad question and suggests a number of others: If censorship is permitted, who should do it? Should universities regulate themselves, or should individual teachers? Should there be different standards for the classroom than, say, for newspapers and television? On what grounds, if any, is censorship permissible—moral, political, military? You will probably find a great variety of opinion among your students on this issue. Even those who adamantly claim to oppose all censorship will regard it as allowable on some grounds; the need to protect national security may sway some, and the need to protect children from violent racist or fascist ideas may sway those on the opposite end of the political spectrum. You may also wish to discuss censorship in history: what can we tell about a society by knowing which ideas certain groups wanted censored? The issue of censorship will be touched on again in Chapter 13 in connection with the spread of the Protestant Reformation, providing an opportunity to renew this discussion.

These are, of course, not the only ways you may choose to broaden a discussion. Because this chapter is comparative, you may want to focus on an issue currently under debate on your campus, exploring its historical roots and perhaps its medieval counterparts.

Sources and Method

Most Western Civilization textbooks include some discussion of medieval universities, but the sources bring up several points that may confuse students and thus require fuller explanation. One of these is the reason that kings and other political authorities granted students special legal status (as the king of France does in Source 1) and freed them from the jurisdiction of secular courts. Clergy in medieval Europe were more or less free from secular jurisdiction, a privilege they had acquired after a long series of struggles between secular rulers and the papacy or other Church officials. (The controversy between Henry II of England and Thomas à Becket is the best example of such a struggle.) Students were not exactly clerics, but because a large share of them were studying for careers in the Church, they were considered to be in "minor orders" and thus entitled to be tried only by other students and clerics. Students did not take vows as priests or members of religious orders did, but they were expected to remain unmarried. (Regulations prohibiting students, or at least undergraduates, from marrying did not end in the Middle Ages, of course. Your students may be surprised to learn that many U.S. colleges had rules forbidding student marriages until after World War II, when the returning soldiers demanded the right to marry while continuing their education.) Given the actions and lifestyles of many medieval students, as evidenced in a number of the sources reprinted in this chapter, this freedom from secular legal jurisdiction was a great bone of contention between the university and the surrounding community.

Medieval sumptuary legislation is another point you may wish to discuss more fully in your introduction to this chapter. Many of the regulations presented here discuss appropriate dress for scholars and specifically forbid certain colors, fabrics, and styles of clothing. Such a public dress code may seem odd to your students, but it was, of course, not unique to universities. Towns frequently passed extensive codes of sumptuary legislation that regulated not only the permissible dress of various social groups but also how much money persons in each social group could spend on functions like weddings, baptisms, and funerals. These codes were intended both to reinforce the distinctions among groups, so that a person's economic and social standing could be known simply by looking at him or her, and to prevent extravagant expenditure, so that people would buy local products rather than imported clothing or food. As you can tell from the specificity of the regulations and the frequency with which they were repeated, students often broke sumptuary laws, dressing in doctor's gowns when they were only bachelors or wearing brightly colored garments. At this point you might mention that academic garb has not changed very much since the Middle Ages and still serves to indicate rank. Bachelor's, master's, and doctor's gowns and hoods are all quite distinct from one another, the doctor's gown and hood being the only ones with velvet ornamentation. The amount of velvet on the gown itself is traditionally limited to three stripes on the sleeves and two front bands, so that medieval doctors could not be mistaken for nobles, who were allowed to wear much more velvet. The colors of the hoods (and sometimes the robes themselves), which identify the wearer's university and degree, serve as a further delineation of status. Though academic garb is reserved for special occasions in the United States, students and teachers at Oxford and Cambridge wear their robes regularly.

A last point that may require some explanation is the way in which medieval students were supported financially. It will be clear to your students from the sources that their medieval counterparts did not hold part-time jobs but depended on their parents or others for financial support. Much of the time this support came from patrons, who gave money to university students as a meritorious act, the type of "good deed" that was their responsibility as Christians. Many patrons were Church officials who supported intelligent young men in part because they hoped to be able to use them as notaries, lawyers, and assistants once their education was completed. Patrons further expected to be mentioned in the dedication of any work their scholars wrote. The actual money for university students came from Church taxes and the income from Church lands throughout Europe. A student might be assigned the income from a specific parish (termed a "living"), though he had no responsibilities in the parish and might in fact have never seen it. Actual parish duties were left in the hands of a vicar or assistant, who often lacked funds for local needs because the money was diverted to the student. Again, Oxford and Cambridge can serve as examples of continuity, for this system continued in England for centuries, surviving the Protestant Reformation and ending only in this century.

The Evidence

Most of the sources are very straightforward, and your students should have little trouble understanding them. An exception may be Source 6, Anselm's proof of the existence of God. This ontological proof, as it is called, involves some specific medieval philosophical notions, the most important of which is that being is always greater than nonbeing. Anselm does not argue that God exists because we can imagine a being such as God, though many of his contemporaries and later commentators thought he was doing so, and they "refuted" this argument by stating that we can imagine a unicorn even though unicorns do not exist. Rather, Anselm argues that "that than which nothing greater can be conceived" (his definition of God) must exist, because if it did not, then something greater could be conceived that did exist. Anselm's awkward phrase makes this a difficult source to discuss, but once your students have captured the reasoning they can have great fun debating his logic.

Sources 7 and 8 may also provoke some confusion, and you may need to discuss Justinian's Code at more length. The code, which came to be called the Corpus Juris Civilis, was compiled by order of the Byzantine emperor Justinian I (483–565); it attempted to systematize Roman law, which had developed incrementally for over a thousand years. Justinian's Code is divided into four parts, the most important of which is the Digest, which contains the laws themselves and commentaries by classical jurists. Numerous editions and copies existed in the West during the Early Middle Ages, but only in the eleventh century, with a revival of interest in Roman law, was this code studied again in western Europe. Its most important commentator was the Italian jurist Irnerius (c. 1055–c. 1130), who is often called the founder of the law school at Bologna that later grew into the university. Jurists trained in Roman law played an important role in the establishment of national legal systems throughout Europe in the early modern period, with the result that Justinian's Code forms the basis of nearly every Continental legal system. Roman law was never introduced into England, which continued to base its legal system on common law. Individual state law codes in the United States are thus also based on common law, except for Louisiana's, which is based on Roman law because the area was initially under the jurisdiction of France.

Depending on the textbook you are using, you may need to provide additional background for the debate about the relation between faith and logic among Christian thinkers in the High Middle Ages, so that students can put Bernard of Clairvaux's comments in Source 9 in context. We have described St. Bernard as a mystic, a term that may be unfamiliar to some of your students. A brief discussion of Christian mysticism, with its ideas of a direct and personal relationship with God through the emotions, may help them better understand Bernard's hostility to Abelard's stress on logic.

You may also wish to mention that the three poems in Source 12 are part of a much larger body of medieval student literature known as Goliardic verse. The term *Goliardic* comes from *Golias*, the name of a mythic giant bishop celebrated in much of this literature for his enormous capacity for wine, women, and song. These poems and songs were written and sung by wandering students and former students, calling themselves Goliards, who upset Church, state, and university officials by their vagrant, unruly life and their flagrant refusal to recognize the benefits of asceticism. The sacrilegious content of their songs, which mimic the form of medieval hymns, further angered Church officials. Your students may have encountered other examples of Goliardic verse in literature classes, for these poems have been widely collected and edited. Students may also have heard many of the poems set to music, particularly the collection called the *Carmina Burana*, a secular cantata written in 1937 with music by Carl Orff.

Questions to Consider

In this section students have two tasks: first, to identify and weigh conflicting opinions about university life; second, to make specific comparisons with their own situation as students. The section notes the distinction between fact and opinion, but you may wish to comment that this distinction is not always clear cut. Students often have the idea that a sharp line divides historical "facts" from later interpretations and opinions, and this would be a good time to point out how little can really be placed in the category of pure fact. This is also a good opportunity to examine how historians weigh the sources they do have and extract the most likely "facts" from them.

This section gives students a number of suggestions to consider when drawing their comparisons, and your best course may simply be to help them follow these guidelines. Your graduate school experience can give you further points of comparison, for in many ways a medieval university was more like a graduate than an undergraduate school; for example, each student was required to have a "master" and was often closely identified with that master.

Epilogue and Evaluation

The epilogue, also comparative, traces some developments within universities from the Middle Ages to today. If you are teaching the entire Western Civilization course, you may wish to return to this chapter when you discuss the student revolts of the 1960s, a topic considered in Chapter 14 of Volume II. How did students view their place in society in 1968, and, conversely, how did society view students, and how did both views compare with those of the twelfth century? (Remember when you are discussing this material that to your students the 1960s may seem as distant as the twelfth century.)

In terms of evaluation, this may be a good chapter for asking your students to do outside work, to discover how their own college or university functions. The second comparative question could then be written up as an essay. You may also wish to set up a debate centering on the final question in Questions to Consider, which focuses on important differences between medieval and modern universities. Another option is to assign an imaginative essay, asking your students to describe a day in the life of a medieval university student. Of course, the central questions may also serve as the basis for a written assignment, or you may simply evaluate the discussion they generate.

For Further Reading

A. B. Cobbam, *The Medieval Universities: Their Development and Organization* (1975). A comprehensive survey of many medieval universities.

Charles Homer Haskins, *The Rise of Universities* (1923). Originally the Colver Lectures at Brown University, this work provides a very brief and lively introduction to many aspects of university life.

Anders Piltz, *The World of Medieval Learning*, trans. David Jones (1981). Provides a general introduction to medieval education from Charlemagne to William of Occam. Nice woodcut illustrations.

Lynn Thorndike, *University Records and Life in the Middle Ages* (1944). A collection of several hundred original sources from universities throughout Europe.

CHAPTER EIGHT
The "Commercial Revolution"

Many of today's students are extremely career conscious and desire a directly relevant and practical college education; for that reason many have chosen to major in business. They often regard liberal arts courses and general education requirements as anachronistic holdovers from an idealistic past or as obstacles to be overcome as quickly as possible, though preferably with a high grade. Some of you may, in fact, teach in required Western Civilization courses, taken by often unenthusiastic students who are convinced this course has nothing to do with their current life or future plans. We hope the material in this chapter will interest them and also surprise those who view business procedures and accounting techniques as extremely modern phenomena. The contracts and other business documents reprinted here demonstrate that—just like states, churches, and other institutions—business has a long history.

Besides providing historical examples of the types of documents your students may be studying in accounting, business, or marketing courses, this chapter has a second—and, in our view, more important—purpose. It is the only chapter that asks students to assess a historical label, to judge the opinions of other historians based on their own reading of documents. As professional historians, we realize that much of our work consists of the revision of labels. We ask such questions as: "Was the Enlightenment truly enlightened?" "Did women have a Renaissance?" "Were the Dark Ages dark?" In this chapter your students will ask, "Was the Commercial Revolution really a revolution?"

The Problem

Content objectives:

1. to learn about new business procedures and types of contracts developed in Italy during the Middle Ages

2. to understand how attitudes toward merchants and toward moneymaking changed in late medieval Europe

3. to identify one of the roots of contemporary capitalism

4. to learn about some of the problems facing medieval merchants and traders

Skills objectives:

1. to understand the terms of a business contract written in formal legal language

2. to realize that historical labels may be reevaluated and perhaps rejected through further research

3. to speculate on writers' own experiences by reading the advice they give to others

In addition to these specific objectives, you may wish to use this chapter as a springboard for discussion of broader questions, such as:

1. Is the Commercial Revolution over—that is, have business procedures been fully rationalized and the role of the merchant totally accepted? At first, your students will probably answer yes. You may want to encourage them to think about such issues as small-town bankers refusing to foreclose on farms despite large debts or the hostility toward middlemen frequently expressed when people learn how small a percentage of the retail price of a food item a farmer actually receives.

2. Why is economic motivation, particularly the drive to make as much money as possible, regarded as rational and modern, whereas other types of motivating forces, such as religion, are considered backward and irrational? This somewhat philosophical question provoked a lengthy and heated discussion in a class comprised mostly of business majors, leading them to think more seriously about the meaning of the word "rational" than they had before. We encouraged them to offer modern examples of decisions and actions by businesspeople that ap-

peared rational or irrational, and this led to further discussion of the role of ethics in business. The topic relates very well to the discussions of honor in many of the sources, particularly to the advice given in Sources 11 and 12.

Sources and Method

Because students are so familiar with banks, corporations, and other facets of modern business life, it may be very difficult for them to envision a world without such institutions—in other words, the medieval world before the Commercial Revolution. Your introduction to this chapter should thus include a discussion of the premarket medieval economy: taxes, debts, and rents usually paid in labor or in kind; villages self-sufficient in basic commodities; a high illiteracy rate among tradespeople, rendering record keeping impossible; roads impassable much of the year because of mud, and unsafe all the time because of robbers; no regular messenger or postal services.

We have discovered that the issue of money takes the most explaining. As economic historians point out and your students should come to understand, money has a number of different functions: it is a measure of value, a means of exchange, and a way to store wealth for future exchange. As long as an object performs one or more of these functions, it is technically "money." Cultures have used a number of different objects as money: the Celts measured value in parts of a milk cow; various African tribes have used cowrie shells as a means of storing wealth; and the merchant in Source 1 of this chapter paid off his debt in pepper. Precious metals perform all three functions very well and so have most often been used as money. Most human cultures have valued these metals because of their scarcity and aesthetic qualities, making them useful both as measures of value and as means of exchange. Gold and silver are also excellent means of storing wealth because they do not rot or decompose.

Using precious metals as money brings problems, however, some of which are mentioned in the chapter. You may wish to discuss these problems further. In large quantities, gold and silver are extremely heavy and awkward to transport, particularly by land. Because there was no agreement about who had the right to mint money in the Middle Ages, coins were frequently melted down, mixed with a base metal such as copper or tin, then reminted. This debasing was difficult to detect, though it is the origin of the custom of biting coins to tell their value. We usually think of this as a way to separate out wooden nickels, but it was actually used to measure the amount of gold in a "gold" coin. Pure gold is very soft, so the deeper the teeth marks, the more valuable the coin. Because the practice of debasing meant that weight was not an accurate indication of a coin's value, merchants and money-changers came to rely on simple visual inspection of the coins they were given. This in turn led to people's shaving or clipping the edges of well-known coins, hoping that no one would notice. The gold and silver shavings could then be used to make additional coins. Gradually the minters of coins began to put mill marks around the edge so that clipped or shaved coins would be detectable. The U.S. dime, quarter, and half dollar still have mill marks, though the "less valuable" penny and nickel do not. All these problems—transport, debasing, and clipping—stem from the fact that medieval coins had intrinsic value, which, of course, most modern coins do not. Their intrinsic value also meant that the value of coins dropped whenever the supply of silver and gold grew, for coins followed the law of supply and demand like any other commodity. You may want to explain this principle here, because you will probably need to come back to it when examining the monetary inflation caused by the discovery of precious metals in the New World and the effects of this inflation on the European and particularly the Spanish economy. (The fact that most modern coinage and paper money have no intrinsic value was clear to our students, but many were still disturbed to learn that modern money systems are based only on the willingness of people to accept different sorts of money as a means of exchange. Your students may be as surprised as ours to learn how little gold there is in Fort Knox and that for all practical purposes the dollar has not been backed by gold since 1970.)

This chapter encourages students to look for signs of economic change in the late medieval period, but you may wish to address the issue of continuities in your introduction. Not only does suspicion of money and merchants continue to be widespread, but much of the money that went to purchase luxury goods and pay for the expenses of transport originally came from agricultural surplus. As the work of Italian economic historians has shown, the Commercial Revolution was initially based on village agriculture and did not emerge outside the manorial system.

The Evidence

The members of your class who have some experience in reading and handling modern contracts will no doubt be pleased by their ready understanding of Sources 1 through 7. For comparative purposes, you could ask one of them to bring in a modern contract, preferably something as simple as a lease. The complexity of its language will no doubt convince the remainder of your class that the contracts reprinted here could not be any more straightforward.

A few features of the evidence may puzzle your students. In Source 3 they will no doubt notice that the two men (who were probably brothers or otherwise related because they have the same last name) invested different amounts yet received equal shares of the profits. This division of profits occurred because Ansaldo, the partner who invested the smaller share, did the actual work for the *societas*, a common arrangement that allowed a younger man to get started in business; in some cases the partner who went on the voyage invested no money at all but received a share simply for his work. The latter was termed the active partner; the one who remained at home was known as the sleeping partner. Recent research on the role of women in international trade has revealed that a large number of women were sleeping partners, particularly in Genoa and Venice. It was not considered socially acceptable for them to be active partners, but they could independently invest money they controlled, particularly their dowries. Source 5 reveals that women investors were not always treated as equals, however, for in this contract the male banker determined what the woman investor's profits would be. It is difficult to imagine a man signing a contract that allowed a banker to return only "what seems to me ought to come to you."

If your students have difficulty understanding the importance of double-entry bookkeeping (the point of having them compare Sources 8 and 9), you might ask them to try totaling the income and outlays in Source 8 the way they are rendered in Source 9. As students add up pence, shillings, and pounds, they will also probably be impressed with the ease of a decimal monetary system and understand why all European countries have finally accepted one (England only recently, of course).

Questions to Consider

The preceding comments will help you guide students through most of the questions in this section, particularly those that arise from the contracts and accounts (Sources 1 through 9). Sources 10 through 14 discuss the activities of merchants but are included primarily to provide evidence of new attitudes among merchants and the development of a "capitalist spirit." They show a group whose values were in flux, for whom it was acceptable to make money but not to flaunt it. You may wish to discuss the reasons for this avoidance of ostentation: Did it develop primarily because the merchants thought money should be reinvested, because they were not used to having large disposable incomes, or because they realized other social groups would resent their new wealth? Sumptuary laws, which we discussed in Chapter 7, also played a role: in many cities merchants were not allowed to wear certain colors or fabrics that were reserved for the nobility. Portraits provide additional evidence that merchants dressed soberly during this period (or at least had their portraits painted in plain clothing); this can best be seen in the portraits of Jacob Fugger (the Rich) and Cosimo de' Medici.

Sources 11 through 14 provide specific advice from medieval merchants for conducting business at home and abroad. Much of this wisdom concerns propriety while living in a strange environment; for those teachers interested in making direct connections to present-day business concerns, a modern advice manual for businesspeople making their first contact with an unfamiliar culture, such as Japan, would provide a good parallel. As you would expect, there are any number of such manuals, as well as consulting firms that advise U.S. companies on protocol, business traditions, and appropriate behavior throughout the world.

Epilogue and Evaluation

The epilogue traces the spread of the new business practices and new attitudes toward merchants from Italy through the rest of Europe, stressing that this was a gradual process. The final paragraph introduces the idea we know as the Weber thesis (the connection between Protestantism and capitalism), although it is not identified by name. Depending on the chronological scope of your course, you may wish to expand on this point here or return to this chapter when you discuss the rise of the Atlantic economies later in the course. In many ways the sources in this chapter can serve as disproof of the Weber thesis, for these Italian Catholic merchants seem imbued by what we would call a "capitalist spirit," a point made by numerous economic historians since Weber. These merchants never regarded financial success as a sign of God's blessing, however, so perhaps to some degree Weber was correct. Judging by portraits, the English and Dutch merchants who are the focus of Weber's thesis agreed with their earlier Italian counterparts that they should "wear modest clothes, be humble, be dull in appearance." You could demonstrate this precept to your class with portraits of early modern Dutch merchants; further, you could make an interesting point about the decline of Italian commerce by comparing these likenesses with portraits of spectacularly dressed Italians such as Lorenzo de' Medici, the grandson of the soberly clad Cosimo.

In evaluating this chapter, you may wish to set up a debate on the central question, "Was there a Commercial Revolution?" This could be based simply on the readings in the chapter or could require additional outside reading. The question could be used as the basis of a written essay, as could the related question, "Which was more important in shaping the later economic development of the West, changes in business procedures or changes in attitudes?"

For Further Reading

Robert-Henri Bautier, *The Economic Development of Medieval Europe* (1971). Designed as an upper-level undergraduate text, with color illustrations.

Cambridge Economic History of Europe, Vols. 1–2 (1941–1966). A good reference for details and for its excellent bibliographies.

Robert S. Lopez, *The Commercial Revolution of the Middle Ages, 950–1350* (1971). A brief survey, intended for undergraduates, that covers all the main points addressed in this chapter.

H. Miskimin, *The Economy of Early Renaissance Europe* (1969). A comprehensive overview of many aspects of economic development during the period.

R. L. Reynolds, *Europe Emerges: Transition Toward an Industrial World-Wide Society, 600–1750* (1961). Puts the Commercial Revolution in a global context by tracing the effects of European developments on other societies. Written for a general audience, with no notes but good maps.

CHAPTER NINE

Craft Guilds: Economic Change and Social Conflict

In the period since World War II, a number of historical "schools" have developed throughout the world, each with a different emphasis. One of the most influential is the Annales school, begun in fact before the war by the French historians Marc Bloch and Lucien Febvre, who in 1929 founded the journal *Annales d'histoire économique et social* (since renamed *Annales: Economies, Sociétés, Civilisation*). Rejecting the traditional concentration on great men and events, Bloch and Febvre sought to create a history that would include all aspects of human life, what they called "total history." The work of Annaliste scholars since then has been marked by a focus on the collective consciousness of groups (termed *mentalité*) rather than the ideas of individuals and on long-term change (*longue durée*) rather than single historical events. Very much in the spirit of the Annales school, this chapter asks students to examine the *mentalité* of craft guild members and to explore how that *mentalité* was transformed over several centuries as economic conditions changed. The period covered by this chapter, the fourteenth through the sixteenth centuries, has been at the center of the research of many Annales historians: Emmanuel Le Roy Ladurie has studied peasants in fourteenth-century southern France (in *Montaillou: The Promised Land of Error*); Philippe Ariés, childhood in early modern France (in *Centuries of Childhood*); and Fernand Braudel, sixteenth-century southern Europe (in *The Mediterranean World in the Age of Philip II*). The chapter also presents many never-before-published sources; original archival research is another hallmark of the Annales school.

The influence of the Annales school is not limited to France but may be seen in the work of many U.S. historians who are part of a movement usually called the "new social history." To the Annales school's emphasis on original sources and long-term change this movement has added methodologies and research techniques developed in other social sciences, particularly quantification from economics and attention to informal social structures from anthropology. Many social historians have also added a focus on women and a concern about the influence of gender on human experience that the Annales school lacked. Following these guidelines, this chapter asks students to consider how the experience of women differed from that of men, a central question in women's history.

The Problem

Content objectives:

1. to learn how craft guilds were established, structured, and organized

2. to examine the role of craft guilds in late medieval and early modern urban life

3. to learn how women's work differed from men's in the guilds

4. to understand how such organizations as guilds responded to economic and social change and why they responded the way they did

5. to learn how social conflict was handled in late medieval and early modern cities and towns

Skills objectives:

1. to understand the language of ordinances and supplications in order to separate formulaic from significant phrases

2. to identify the underlying group concerns that emerge in specific laws; in other words, to determine the reasons that certain laws were passed

3. to extract specific information from a source that discusses a wide variety of issues

4. to use inductive reasoning to draw conclusions about the collective consciousness of a social group

You may also wish to use this chapter as the basis for a discussion of larger issues raised by Annales school methodology and philosophy. One such issue is periodization. We have, of course, inherited our tripartite periodization of Western history (ancient, medieval, modern) from Renaissance historians, who concentrated on political change and great individuals, the very factors the Annales school rejected. The Annales school's emphasis on long-term social and economic change meant that the end of the Roman Empire and the Renaissance and Reformation could no longer be regarded as the decisive breaks they had seemed to be to more traditional historians; nevertheless, the tripartite division was difficult to eradicate. One nuance was added by dividing the modern period into "early modern" and "modern," though this division led to disagreements about when the "early modern" period ended and the real "modern" period began: The French Revolution?—but this was political periodization again. The Industrial Revolution?—but this happened at different times in different parts of Europe. Many of the developments the Annalistes were interested in took centuries to unfold, making necessary such complicated phrases as "late medieval and early modern," a tongue twister we have been forced to use in this chapter as well. The question all of this raises is not simply whether the standard periodization is wrong but whether any periodization makes much sense in terms of "total history." Won't the continuities always be stronger than the disjunctions? Women's history also calls traditional periodization into question, for major changes in the lives of some groups of men have often brought no change to the lives of women. (Chapters 2 and 11 both introduce another issue in periodization, that of value labels such as "Golden Age" and "Renaissance." Because the basic tripartite division is a product of the Renaissance, you may wish to refer again to your discussion of periodization when you reach Chapter 11.)

Another issue raised by Annales historiography, directly related to the central question of this chapter, is whether we can ever really understand the *mentalité* of an entire group of people, particularly a group that lived five hundred years ago. Detractors of the Annalistes point out that this search for collective consciousness tends to ignore individual ideas that differed from those more commonly held; and further, they argue, the search is ultimately futile because the most basic ideas of any group are precisely those that are never explicitly stated. An idea that is unquestioningly accepted and cherished by all does not need frequent reinforcement, the critics contend, and for that reason it leaves no historical trace. They note that anthropologists frequently question how well outsiders can understand another culture, because some information is never shared with outsiders; similarly, they caution, historians should be careful about claiming to understand the totality of any culture because "the past is a foreign country." (The phrase is the title of David Lowenthal's recent book that questions how well we can ever understand the past.)

Once your students have completed their analysis of the sources for this chapter, you may wish to play devil's advocate and ask them to defend their conclusions. How can they be sure they are not misinterpreting the evidence? How can they accurately reconstruct the attitudes of long-dead people? Do groups really have a *mentalité*? (To help students think about this issue, you might ask them to describe those attitudes of their peer group they would classify as part of a general consciousness, and then ask them to think about which surviving sources might convey this consciousness to historians five hundred years from now. This exercise may also help them understand the adage that the most widely held beliefs leave no traces behind.)

Sources and Method

Many standard Western Civilization texts include surprisingly little historical information about craft guilds, so we have provided a somewhat longer than normal introduction. This introduction includes the background we believe is necessary to understand the sources, but to assist your students in answering this chapter's questions you may wish to emphasize the following points: The guilds grew up in cities that were usually already centers of trade, with a political and economic leadership made up of merchants and bankers (thus the developments in this chapter follow those discussed in the last chapter causally as well as chronologically). The guilds were therefore never totally independent but always under the jurisdiction of a city council made up initially of those merchants and bankers. As the introduction points out, guild members in some cities eventually joined the merchants on the city council and other urban government institutions, but the merchants still retained a dominant voice. Because merchants' guilds did not set upper limits on the amount of trade any member could handle but restricted their members' level of production, trade rather than production offered individuals the opportunity to become extremely wealthy.

The guilds were urban institutions, and their fortunes rose and fell with those of their parent cities. All guild members were required to be citizens of the town in which they worked. This meant that their hostility toward nonmembers was often translated into a hostility toward or at least suspicion of noncitizens. Citizenship brought both responsibilities and privileges. Citizens were expected to repair city fortifications, pay taxes, serve in the citizens' militia, and act as night watchmen; in turn, they were generally favored by their city's law courts in suits involving noncitizens. Noncitizens residing in a city had to register in the same way that resident aliens do in the United States today and could be forced to leave at any time.

Women as well as men were counted and described as citizens, and they could often pass along their citizenship to noncitizen husbands; exactly what this citizenship entailed, however, is unclear. One historian has described women of this period as having "passive citizenship" because they did not perform military duty; the problem with this definition is that older male citizens also did not serve in the citizens' militia but sent substitutes in the same way that female heads of household did. Women who were heads of households were required to pay all taxes that male heads of household paid and assist as well in the repair of fortifications. In general, it appears that female citizens had all the responsibilities of male citizens, few of the privileges, and none of the political rights. As far as we know, women never served on a city council or in any other political capacity other than as gatekeepers, jail wardens, market inspectors, and similarly minor functionaries.

The gender differences in citizenship parallel the differences in the guilds in many ways. As your students can see from the readings, women were present in guild shops but only rarely as official participants in the guild structure. The widows who maintained shops after their husbands died paid all guild dues but never served as overseers or as leaders in a guild. Though we cannot know for sure, they probably did not march along with the rest of the guild in urban processions, an act that was an important symbol of guild solidarity. The few all-female guilds were often under male leadership as well, as your students can tell from Source 3.

Guilds that felt threatened often tried to limit the number of workshops. As the sources indicate, this often meant restrictions on widows and women workers. The women then turned to the city council (Sources 10 and 11), which might well grant their requests and serve as their "protector" because women's or other nonguild labor was no threat to the wealthy merchants and bankers who made up the majority of the council. This pattern, of course, has continued for centuries. The groups showing the most hostility to those perceived as outsiders are those at the bottom of the insiders' social and economic scale. Those at the top can afford to be magnanimous and talk about opportunities for all because their livelihood is not threatened. (You may wish to make some comparisons between the guilds' restrictiveness and suspicion of women and the attitude displayed until very recently by the modern labor movement, although this is a touchy issue in many parts of the United States.)

The disputes between guilds and city councils about who could work in or run a shop were part of the larger power struggle between these two groups to determine the economic policies of the city. Because of the rivalry, such conflicts were often viewed as symbolically important and for that reason were more bitterly fought than one would expect. This is also true for the fights between masters and journeymen about who could work in a shop; neither side wanted to grant the other the power to make this decision, because it might lead to the claiming of other powers.

The Evidence

The chapter discusses at some length the distinction between prescriptive and descriptive sources, so you may need only to touch on this point to be sure your students have grasped the distinction. The ordinances (Sources 1 through 8) are written in very plain language, and your students should not have any difficulty determining what problems the guilds hoped to solve in each one. They may need some direction in evaluating why certain matters were viewed as problems, and what this attitude reveals about the mind-set of the guild masters.

The language of the supplications (Sources 10 and 11) is very flowery, with many phrases added to flatter the city council or persuade it to look on the supplicant as especially pitiful and worthy of special consideration. One would probably expect such language in supplications, and many of these phrases are simply formulaic. (This might be a good place to mention the importance and function of formulaic phrases.)

Most of the evidence in this chapter is published here for the first time; none of it was "published" at the time it was written. Particularly if your own research has included the use of unpublished documents, you may wish to discuss how archives are used and some of the problems archival research entails. In our experience, most students have never really considered the fact that all original sources from before 1450 are handwritten, nor what problems there might be in simply deciphering them. Chapter 5 on the Domesday Book provided a taste of this, and we have also introduced copies of handwritten sources from our own research for further illustration. The sight of these densely covered pages may have dissuaded some students from further research in history, but most of them now appreciate how much real "discovery" occurs in research that uses original sources.

Questions to Consider

In Sources and Method, students are directed to make a three-column list of the changes the guilds viewed as problems, the solutions they proposed, and the probable reasons for their views. In this section, students are asked to evaluate their lists to arrive at some conclusions about the *mentalité* of the guilds. Answering the questions in this chapter involves more speculation than in other chapters, but this is to be expected, given the nature of the questions. You can help your students by asking them to consider why different groups of people in any society would view certain changes as a threat. Were they a direct economic threat? A threat to the group's political power? A threat to the group's social standing?

It is important for students to see that the conflicts explored in this chapter—between guilds and city councils, between guild masters and journeymen—were not simply about economic issues or political power but also involved social status and honor. In the contemporary United States, social and economic status tend to be closely linked, but this was not so in the period discussed here. Family background was an important determinant of status (a fact that your students have probably picked up from the role of families in these sources), as was personal honor. Certain occupations, such as grave-digging, managing brothels, and executing criminals, were regarded as dishonorable, though their practitioners could be quite wealthy. For the journeymen, working alongside women came to be regarded as dishonorable, so they fought women in the shops even when this hostility worked to their own economic disadvantage. They would not allow their wives to work alongside them, so the wives had to take lower-paying employment outside the guild economy. Similarly, when a master died, journeymen often quit working in the shop to avoid working for a woman, even when this meant unemployment.

Because of the role of noneconomic issues, it is hard to use a clear-cut class analysis when examining the conflicts discussed here. That is why we have put the words "middle class" in quotes in the central questions. You may wish to use this point as a springboard for a discussion of the transformation of European society from a society of "orders" (what the Germans call *Stande*) to a class society, a transformation that began during the period covered in this chapter and involved many of the economic and social issues mentioned here.

Epilogue and Evaluation

The epilogue continues the discussion of developments in the organization of production, giving a brief overview of the stages of capitalism. We have chosen to ignore the great debate between economic historians and labor historians about the most important factor in the origins of capitalism; we have simply commented that both trade and production play a part. By stressing that capitalism developed and craft guilds endured over centuries, we have again taken an Annales school approach emphasizing long-term change.

Because this chapter involves more speculation and inductive reasoning than some of the others, this might be a good time to assign a written project, asking students to defend their analysis of the *mentalité* of the craft guilds with specific examples from the sources. In this way, you can stress that even the most creative historical reconstruction must be based on a clear understanding of the surviving evidence.

For Further Reading

The general surveys of medieval economic history mentioned in the preceding chapter all discuss craft guilds. In addition, you may wish to consult:

Joseph and Francis Gies, *Life in a Medieval City* (1969). A very basic discussion of life in a prosperous northwest European city during the twelfth and thirteenth centuries, using Troyes in Champagne as an example. Designed as a monograph to be used by beginning students.

Barbara Hanawalt (ed.), *Women's Work in Pre-Industrial Europe* (1987). A collection of essays examining a number of different types of women's work in both the rural and urban economies.

Martha Howell, "Citizenship and Gender: Women's Political Status in Northern European Medieval Cities," in *Women and Power in the Middle Ages,* ed. Mary Erler and Maryanne Kowaleski (1988). Discusses the connections between women's role in the craft guilds and their role as citizens.

Henri Pirenne, *Economic and Social History of Medieval Europe* (1936). The classic summary by the great Belgian medieval historian. Also see his *Medieval Cities* (1956) for a discussion of the role of trade in urban development.

Merry Wiesner, *Women's Work in Renaissance Germany* (1986). Devotes one section specifically to changes in women's work in the craft guilds during the fifteenth and sixteenth centuries.

CHAPTER TEN

Lay Piety and Heresy in the Late Middle Ages

During the past twenty years, popular culture has increasingly become a recognized field of study for literary scholars, art historians, music historians, and sociologists. The Popular Culture Society holds regular scholarly meetings, and its members no longer have to defend their interests quite as much to their more traditional colleagues. The great bulk of research into popular culture has examined the contemporary scene, or the early twentieth century at the earliest, but now historians of much earlier periods have begun to explore the beliefs, rituals, and traditions of common people, slowly building an understanding of the popular culture of more distant times. They, too, have often had to justify their interests, to assert that what they are studying is truly history and not folklore or some kind of second-class "folk history." (The distinction between "history" and "folk history" is the sharpest in Germany, where the two are often separate academic departments.) As our understanding of earlier popular culture has deepened, increasingly we have seen the connections between popular and elite culture and have realized that the lines of influence run both ways. Especially in the premodern period, even the most highly educated individuals participated in popular rituals and lived in a mental world shaped by folk beliefs.

This chapter explores one aspect of late medieval popular culture, the religious beliefs and practices of laypeople, both those accepted by the Church as orthodox and those it judged heretical. We are careful never to call these customs and beliefs "superstitions" or to trivialize them; rather, we recognize that any way in which people choose to understand and express their religious faith is legitimate. Lay Christians turned to those aspects of Christianity that met their own spiritual needs, occasionally mixing in pre-Christian beliefs and ideas as well. The original missionaries to much of Europe had built on preexisting pagan religions to win converts, so this was not simply the result of the common people's misunderstanding of Christianity. Many highly complex doctrines, such as the Trinity and the dual nature of Christ, were not defined by theologians and Church officials until centuries after the time of Christ. Most lay Christians probably did not follow a totally orthodox interpretation of such doctrines because these were not the most important features of Christianity to them. Further, the institutional Church was only occasionally interested in how people understood official doctrines. Only when a group's interpretations led it to break from Rome or criticize the clergy, or especially when heterodox interpretations led to a decline in Church revenues, did Church officials grow concerned. Rigid doctrinal orthodoxy of the kind imposed by the nineteenth- and early-twentieth-century Roman Catholic Church was rarely insisted on by the medieval Church.

The Problem

Content objectives:

1. to examine the beliefs and practices of lay Christians in the late Middle Ages

2. to learn why certain aspects of Christianity held more popular appeal than others

3. to learn the reasons for popular criticism of the institutional Church

4. to understand why the Church as an institution felt threatened by some lay religious ideas

Skills objectives:

1. to assess how the intent of a written document shapes the way it is written

2. to describe religious beliefs and practices in objective terms

3. to see how alternative beliefs reflect people's dissatisfaction with existing religious institutions

4. to integrate visual evidence, oral testimony, and written documents

In addition to these specific skills, you may wish to use this chapter to initiate a general discussion about the ways in which we study popular culture and about the interplay between popular and elite culture in any society. (We have intentionally avoided frequent use of the term *popular* in the chapter itself because of the word's many meanings. Here we use it to mean "belonging to the common people" rather than "prevalent" or "widely approved.") Once your students have worked through this chapter, you may ask them to think about parallel sources that reveal the beliefs and attitudes of contemporary Americans. What sorts of places of pilgrimage have replaced or supplemented religious ones? (Examples such as the Statue of Liberty, the Vietnam War Memorial, Graceland mansion, and the Gettysburg battlefield may help start them thinking.) What do these latter-day shrines reveal about the change in popular attitudes since the Middle Ages? What types of miracles do contemporary preachers mention in their sermon stories to encourage certain behavior? What sorts of contemporary images function, as the crucifix and the Virgin Mary did in the Middle Ages, as visual reminders of faith or beliefs?

These questions may encourage your students at first to compare medieval and contemporary popular culture in overly dichotomous terms; for instance, medieval popular culture was religious and spiritual, whereas contemporary popular culture is secular and materialistic. If they do so, you may wish to introduce other evidence of various religious aspects of modern popular culture: the huge numbers of pilgrims at Lourdes, for example, or the weeping image of the Virgin Mary in a Catholic church in south Chicago, to say nothing of the miracle healings of television evangelists.

Sources and Method

In many ways, the students' own work in Chapter 4, "The Development of Orthodoxy in Early Christianity," provides them with the best background for this chapter. In that chapter they explored how Christianity established a canonical text of the New Testament, a simple statement of beliefs in the Apostles' Creed, and a body of authority in the bishops, allowing the Church to define orthodoxy and become a unified, powerful institution. They also traced early examples of people who disagreed with orthodox interpretations and with the establishment of a hierarchy of power within the Church. By the late Middle Ages, criticism of both the doctrines and the structure of the Church had become extremely strong again; ideas and institutions that had been established for more than a millennium came under increased attack.

Your own introduction to this chapter might include a brief summary of the history and organization of the medieval Church, if the textbook you are using does not discuss this subject adequately. Students should understand the distinction between regular and secular clergy and be aware that most parish priests did not preach sermons but left that task to wandering monks and friars. These monks often became extremely popular; people abandoned their own parish services and flocked from miles around to hear them. The competition between parish priests and monks often led each group to support laypeople's resentments of the other; thus Source 2, the sermon story in which a priest is described as "wily," was probably originally told by a monk.

You may also need to stress the fact that lower-level clergy, particularly parish priests, often had no share in the great wealth of the Church but were as poor as their parishioners. They frequently had to farm the parish lands six days a week, serving as priests only on Sundays. This was one of the reasons that many priests married or had concubines, despite official prohibitions; not only did women provide companionship, they also assisted in running the parish household, preparing food, making clothing, and caring for the animals. Because parish clergy were supported by obligatory tithes from their parishioners, they bore the brunt of lay resentment against the Church. At the same time, priests had to pay an income tax to the papacy and often various fees to higher-level Church officials, leading them to share their parishioners' resentment of the Church's financial demands. Criticism of the institutional Church was not simply a lay phenomenon in the late Middle Ages but was entrenched in clergy at many levels as well. For this reason and others, most laypeople did not turn away from the Church but hoped to reform it.

Another facet of late medieval piety that may need further explanation is the cult of the Virgin. During the Early Middle Ages, Christian missionaries and theologians tended to downplay the role of Mary in order to distinguish Christianity from pre-Christian classical and Germanic religions that had female deities. Once Christianity became the official religion of most of Europe—about the eleventh century—Mary began to figure more prominently in sermons, stories, and worship practices. Religious orders and confraternities dedicated to Mary were established; huge numbers of churches and cathedrals were erected in her name. (In Germany, many of these churches were built on the sites of former Jewish ghettos as towns and cities banished Jewish residents and confiscated their property.) The devotion to Mary clearly evident in the sources in this chapter spread beyond the uneducated people; it was shared by such highly educated churchmen as Bernard of Clairvaux. The Marian cult became even more widespread in the later Middle Ages, when preachers tended to stress the judgmental and divine aspects of Christ, leading people to feel a greater need for the nurturing qualities of Mary as compensation.

Though we might expect that worship of Mary would lead to an improvement in the status of women, such was not the case; in fact, the opposite may have been true. Mary was viewed as so extraordinary that normal women could never hope to emulate her; instead, they remained much more closely identified with Eve, who was judged by many theologians to be solely responsible for original sin. Because women represented the greatest temptation to the churchmen who had devoted themselves to Mary, the same sermons that praised Mary often denigrated or vilified all other women, and the Church as an institution became extremely misogynist. Thus a figure like

Margery Kempe, or even Bridget of Sweden, was suspect not only because she was a layperson who saw visions and felt a special call from God, but even more because she was a woman.

The Evidence

Your general introduction to the medieval Church and the cult of Mary should be all students need to understand the first five sources, though you may also wish to mention Christian attitudes toward Jews as background to the story of the image of St. Nicholas in Source 3. This might be a good place, if you have not done so already in the course, to mention the economic roots of Christian anti-Semitism and the way in which such stories reinforced stereotypes.

To understand the heresy trial records (Sources 6 and 7), your students need some groundwork in basic Christian beliefs. The direct comparison of Roman Catholic orthodoxy to Albigensian beliefs in Source 6 has been included for this reason, but you may find that the concepts of purgatory, penance, sacrament, and the like require further explanation. Do not rely on your students' own word that they understand Christian doctrine; we have found that even students at colleges with church affiliations often have very fuzzy or incorrect notions. If many of your students are Protestant fundamentalists, you will also need to explain the Catholic Church's position on the equal weight of Scripture and tradition—that is, that not all doctrines accepted as orthodox may be found in the Bible. (You may be surprised, as we were, at the strength of anti-Catholic sentiment among some young people today. That is why we have included the phrase "in objective terms" in our skills objectives list; you may need to caution students about the use of words such as "cult" or "superstition.")

In analyzing the two sculptures (Sources 8 and 9), encourage students to examine the facial expressions of the Virgin and of Christ. The Madonna has been depicted in a number of ways throughout history; this version is called the "Queen of Heaven" because of the royal regalia. Portraying Mary as a queen in this manner was a very common practice at the time that numerous cathedrals dedicated to her were being erected. It is easy to understand the motivation, given the respect for royalty in medieval Europe; but this kind of image made Mary appear less approachable than when she was portrayed in other ways—for example, as the "Mother of Sorrows" mourning over her son. As a consequence, believers increasingly offered their prayers and supplications to Mary's mother Anne, asking her as an approachable female figure to intercede for them with God. The manner in which Christ is portrayed has also changed over the centuries; sometimes the crucifix has held an ethereal figure little troubled by his fate, and at other times, as in this sculpture, a very human, suffering form. The late Middle Ages was a period of doubt and uncertainty in many areas of life, a despair reflected even in the portrayal of Christ.

Questions to Consider

In this section students are asked to sort through the information they have uncovered, to separate lay beliefs from the official Church reaction to them. Your discussion of the cult of Mary should help them answer the questions about Mary's important role in lay piety; the statue showing her as the Queen of Heaven is a good indication that in the minds of many people she was not simply the mother of Christ but a goddess. Two of the attitudes that both orthodox thinkers and heretics shared were distaste for the Church's wealth and the sense that Christ could appear directly to lay believers. As your students have no doubt gathered from the readings, the Church was often more concerned about the former than about the latter, particularly when hostility to clerical wealth led to an actual decrease in Church revenues. The Church was often suspicious of those who had visions or other direct experiences of God, particularly if they were women, because these revelations reduced the individual's dependence on priests and the sacraments; however, the Church never condemned mystical experiences outright. The financial concerns of the Church hierarchy can be seen most clearly in the way it dealt with the Albigensians. Many Albigensian beliefs differed sharply from those of orthodox Christianity, much more so than those of the Lollards; indeed, it is difficult really to call the Albigensians Christian, a point you may wish to discuss with your students. It was not, however, until the movement became widely popular—and Church income from the wealthy part of southern France, where the sect was spreading, fell off precipitously—that the papacy took the Albigensians seriously, sent inquisitors, and, eventually, called a crusade against them. Theological heterodoxy alone was often not enough to warrant repression by the Church.

The same factors can be seen in the fate of other medieval heretical movements, such as that begun by Peter Waldo. Waldo called on the Church to give all its wealth to the poor, and his followers were initially persecuted in the French towns where the movement began. Once the Waldensians fled from urban society into the Swiss Alps, the Church more or less forgot them because they no longer posed an economic or political threat. Isolated in mountain valleys, they clung to their own beliefs and practices until they joined with the Protestants several centuries later. The Protestant Reformation itself provides another example: the pope regarded the whole affair with Luther as a monks' quarrel, a dispute between the Augustinians and Dominicans, until his income was threatened by Luther's crusade against indulgences.

Epilogue and Evaluation

The epilogue places the lay piety movement in the late Middle Ages within the context of other developments in the medieval Church, particularly the Great Schism, and notes that it is one of the many factors that led to the Protestant Reformation. You may wish to return to this chapter when you begin to answer the questions in Chapter 13, especially the second question on the eagerness of the common people to hear the message of the Protestant reformers.

The most creative way to evaluate this chapter may be to treat these sources as the foundation for mock interviews. Ask your students to draw up a list of questions they wish to ask Margery Kempe, Bridget, an Albigensian, or a Lollard, or perhaps even the inquisitors of these figures. On the basis of the information in the sources, how would each of these individuals answer the questions? You may wish to perform the interviews as a role play, with some class members taking the part of the historical figures quoted in the chapter, basing their answers on what they already know about each person's beliefs and personality. If your class enjoys role playing, you could also set this up as an inquisition, a format that would help students see how the form of the questions shapes the answers. (We advise you to skip the torture, although doubtless some members of your class would be happy to describe medieval methods of torture quite explicitly. Somehow there is always one student in every class who has done extensive research on this subject.)

For Further Reading

Clarissa W. Atkinson, *Mystic and Pilgrim: The Book and World of Margery Kempe* (1983). The best recent biography, which also discusses Kempe's milieu and the history of her autobiography.

Norman Cohn, *The Pursuit of the Millennium: Revolutionary Millenarians and Mystical Anarchists of the Middle Ages* (1961). An excellent discussion of a number of small heretical groups and their leaders.

Jaroslav Pelikan, *Jesus Through the Ages: His Place in the History of Culture* (1985). An analysis of the way in which Jesus has been portrayed in words and images. Wonderful illustrations and examples from all over the world.

Barbara Tuchman, *A Distant Mirror: The Calamitous Fourteenth Century* (1978). A wide-ranging discussion of the century by one of the best contemporary popular historians. Designed for a general audience, yet not overly simplistic.

Marina Warner, *Alone of All Her Sex: The Myth and the Cult of the Virgin Mary* (1978). The most comprehensive analysis of Marian beliefs and worship practices.

CHAPTER ELEVEN

The Renaissance Man and Woman

Few periods in history have been as romanticized as the Renaissance—or have been subjected in recent years to as much revisionist analysis. Medievalists have pointed to the strong continuities between Renaissance and medieval culture as well as to the medieval revivals in learning, similar to those of the Renaissance, that occurred during the ninth century under Charlemagne and during the twelfth century with the founding of the universities. Medievalists have labeled these earlier movements "renaissances" as well, denying the historical uniqueness of the changes instituted by Petrarch and the other Italian humanists. Historians of science have observed that the Renaissance was not a period of scientific advance and may actually have represented a decline from the level of knowledge achieved in the Middle Ages, because truth was sought in ancient texts rather than in laboratory experiments; scientific discoveries usually attributed to the Renaissance, such as those in astronomy and anatomy, were in fact products of a later period. According to economic historians, the Renaissance was a period of absolute or at least relative decline for precisely those northern Italian cities most often linked with its efflorescence. Social historians, stressing the elite nature of Renaissance culture, note that for most Europeans the fourteenth century was a time of calamity rather than rebirth. Women's historians have demonstrated that even upper-class women rarely participated in the new learning or artistic endeavors and, as students will discover in this chapter, were not included in the new conceptions about the ultimate meaning and purpose of human life.

Despite all these changes in our picture of that period, most historians would still agree that something called the "Renaissance" did happen and that in many ways the ideas of Jacob Burckhardt, as expressed in his *The Civilization of the Renaissance in Italy*, first published in 1860, remain the starting point for any discussion of the period. The qualities that Burckhardt stressed as central to Renaissance culture—classicism, individualism, secularism—were quite distinct from those of medieval culture and, though rarely achieved in actuality, expressed at least ideals that some upper-class men hoped to attain. This chapter therefore explores the ideals that Renais-

80

sance thinkers proposed for men, women, and rulers as simply that—ideals—rather than asking students to compare ideals with reality, as they did for classical Athens in Chapter 2. The chapter views the Renaissance as its chief participants and proponents did—as an intellectual movement—thus concentrating on the one sphere in which both traditionalists and revisionists would agree that significant change did occur.

The Problem

Content objectives:

1. to learn about humanist ideals of education for boys and girls

2. to trace the development of humanism from classical to courtly

3. to understand Renaissance ideas about the proper roles for rulers and courtiers and about the nature of political leadership

4. to learn about Renaissance conceptions of the physical and mental qualities of the ideal man and woman

Skills objectives:

1. to apply a general understanding of the culture of a historical period to an analysis of its art

2. to read biographies and autobiographies for the subject's beliefs as well as details of his or her life

3. to compare the ideals held up by various authors and artists

4. to use the separate ideals set out for men and women as a tool in understanding the role of gender in determining human experience

Besides these specific objectives, you may wish to use this chapter as a springboard to a broader discussion of the role of new ideals in bringing about historical change. Can (or did) new ideals change human behavior? Do ideals matter? Do they matter only to the elite? Do nonelites create their own ideals, and, if so, how are they different from those of the elites? You may also wish to expand the discussion by asking your students to consider how the ideals expressed in these sources have been maintained or altered since the Renaissance, a point made in the epilogue. Can they find modern examples of the idealization of the same qualities for men, women, and rulers in advertising or political speeches? Are the connections between the Middle Ages and the Renaissance weak enough to warrant calling the Renaissance the beginning of the modern era, or is it best viewed as a separate epoch?

Sources and Method

Most Western Civilization textbooks provide a good discussion of what might best be termed the "classic" view of the Renaissance, and many have also begun to incorporate some revisionist views, so you should not have to provide as much factual background for this chapter as you have for many of the other chapters. You do need to be sure, however, that your students have a clear idea of what "humanism" and "secularism" mean in the context of the Renaissance. We have pointed out that these terms did not carry the same meaning then as they do in modern usage, and that they were generally seen as positive qualities; but you may wish to reinforce our discussion, especially if you teach in a part of the country where "humanism" is seen as the first step on the path to godless communism. (Similarly, you may wish to emphasize, as we have, that the meaning of the word "liberal" for Renaissance educational theorists bears little relation to its current political usage.)

For your students to put the written sources in perspective, you may need to provide additional background in two areas. The first is medieval education, because it is impossible to understand the innovations of the humanist program of study without knowing how education was conceptualized and organized in the Middle Ages. Here you may wish to review the class discussions of Chapter 7, especially those relating to the content of higher education. The second area consists of the political and military developments in fifteenth- and early-sixteenth-century Italy, especially the French invasions and the gradual transformation of most Italian city-states into principalities. Knowledge of these events will help your students understand the change from classical to courtly humanism and provide them with the historical background for the writings of Castiglione and Machiavelli.

You may use this chapter for comparative analysis in several ways, either before your students tackle the central questions or after they have finished. One comparison, between the instructional programs of medieval universities discussed in Chapter 7 and the humanist programs discussed in this chapter, has already been mentioned. A second comparison, between the ideals for human behavior established by the ancient Athenians (Chapter 2) and those in this chapter, would also be appropriate, especially because the Renaissance thinkers were consciously attempting to emulate the ancient world. This exercise could be carried out using either general ideas about proper male and female behavior and qualities or more specific concepts, such as Plato's guardians and Machiavelli's prince. Such a discussion would provide a good lead-in to a more general discussion of the degree to which the Renaissance represented, on one hand, a true rebirth of classical culture and, on the other hand, a totally new intellectual movement. That topic would tie in with the questions posed in Questions to Consider about the effects of the social and political background of ideas. Once your students have answered a question for Renaissance Italy such as "How might political changes have affected the ideals proposed for rulers?" they could proceed to a comparative question, such as "What political and social developments might have prevented Renaissance thinkers from sharing the ideals of Plato or Aristotle despite their respect for these philosophers?"

Though initially favoring a republican form of government, Petrarch and other Renaissance thinkers came to admire Julius Caesar and Augustus as leaders who exhibited the prize quality of *virtu*. You could thus use Chapter 3 for comparison as well, posing such questions as "What achievements of Augustus would Renaissance thinkers have particularly celebrated?" You may also wish to ask your students to consider other historical figures they have studied in the course who have not been specifically mentioned in *Discovering the Western Past*. Who else would they regard as exhibiting *virtu*—Akhenaton, perhaps? Charlemagne? Joan of Arc? Mentioning Joan in this context, of course, provokes the question of whether a woman can exhibit *virtu*, a quality the Renaissance thinkers viewed as quintessentially masculine. (The word itself, related to the Latin word for "man," is, in fact, often translated as "manliness.") A contemporary of many of the writers in this chapter, Joan disturbed both her French supporters and her English captors as much by her masculine dress as by her military actions and her claim of hearing divine voices. Discussing her life briefly here would be a good way to emphasize the fact that Renaissance ideals were extremely gender specific.

The Evidence

Art historians may cringe at the way we have directed students to examine the three portraits. They may regard the questions as overly directive and perhaps anachronistic: can one really assume that certain facial expressions conveyed the same qualities in the Renaissance that they do now? Art historians may also argue that these three portraits represent extreme examples, that not all art in the Renaissance was secular, that only Dürer portrayed himself as Christ and only the *condottieri* had themselves portrayed by sculptors and painters in the dynamic way Colleoni is rendered here. We recognize these limitations but would say in reply that such features illustrate the innovations of the Renaissance, which is what students are investigating in the chapter. In any period of major artistic change, most paintings and sculptures do not follow the new styles but remain "traditional" (however that term is defined) in technique and subject matter. The few that do change are the focus of our attention. (Who, for example, pays much attention to French historical paintings of the late nineteenth century except as an example of a genre and style the impressionists reacted against?)

Further, we have chosen the portraits by Dürer and Botticelli not only because they represent such good illustrations of ideal types but because both artists were highly involved in the philosophical movements of the Renaissance. As your textbook may mention, and as you should point out to your students, Botticelli shared the Neoplatonic ideas of Leonardo Bruni and Lorenzo de' Medici, a philosophical school that emphasized the links between earthly and divine beauty. (Later in his life, under the influence of Savonarola, Botticelli rejected this stance; his last paintings return to religious subjects and are very somber in tone.) Dürer, a member of a humanist discussion group in Nuremberg, traveled to Italy as a young man, where he came into contact not only with Italian art but also with Italian humanist philosophy. Though the work of some artists may to some extent be understood outside the social context in which they worked, the work of these two cannot.

Sources 4 through 8, which discuss ideals straightforwardly, should be easy for your students to handle on their own. You may, however, need to provide some assistance in drawing out abstract concepts from Alberti's and Vergil's purportedly biographical descriptions. Perhaps the easiest way for your students to identify the ideals here is to have them try to match the personal characteristics mentioned with the ideals discussed in Sources 4 through 8. Alberti, for example, describes himself as "educated liberally . . . assiduous in dealing with arms and horses." Where have they seen these qualities mentioned before? Negative qualities may also be part of both idealizations and descriptions. For example, both Machiavelli and Vergil believe that avarice is the worst trait a ruler can possess, though Machiavelli expresses this view directly and Vergil by noting that it was Henry VII's greatest flaw.

Questions to Consider

The questions posed in the first paragraph of this section compare the ideas of the writers and are best used to stimulate class discussion. There are no right or wrong responses; answering these questions requires only a careful reading of the sources. The next set of questions asks for a comparison of the authors' broader assumptions and thus calls for a bit more speculation, though your students should easily discern the fact that Machiavelli, in striking contrast to most Renaissance humanists, held a negative opinion of human nature.

The questions relating to the social and political origins of Renaissance ideas incorporate information provided by your textbook and by your own introduction to this chapter. Here again, material from an earlier chapter may be fruitfully introduced. The wealth derived from the increase in trade and commerce discussed in Chapter 8, for example, provided the material basis for the flourishing of Renaissance culture. Likewise, the primacy of Italian merchants in the Commercial Revolution is one reason that the Renaissance began in Italy (though it is not, of course, the only reason). Your students will need some information on Castiglione's and Machiavelli's personal careers to assess how their life experiences might have affected their ideas. This background may be provided in your text; if not, you should briefly mention that Castiglione had an illustrious career in the service of a number of different rulers, whereas Machiavelli was exiled by the Medicis when they regained power in Florence because he had served the republican government. *The Prince* may, in fact, have been written as an attempt to ingratiate himself again with the Medicis, though this interpretation is disputed.

Epilogue and Evaluation

The epilogue asks students to consider how the ideals they have just examined spread geographically and socially; it discusses both the ways in which the Renaissance represented a new era and the ways in which this period was connected to the medieval past. You may wish to point out that because the Renaissance constituted an intellectual change rather than a historical event, it "happened" at different times in different places.

For purposes of evaluation, this chapter is well suited to the assignment of a paper that incorporates material from previous chapters. Any of the several suggestions for comparisons already made could be turned into a written assignment, and there are a variety of other ways in which to frame comparative questions. These questions could look forward as well as backward by asking students to compare contemporary ideals with those held by the Renaissance authors in this chapter.

For Further Reading

Jacob Burckhardt, *The Civilization of the Renaissance in Italy* (1958). A tremendously influential work since its first publication in 1860, this book sets the terms for all later analyses of the Renaissance.

Joan Kelly Gadol, "Did Women Have a Renaissance?" in Renate Bridenthal and Claudia Koonz, *Becoming Visible: Women in European History* (1977). An extremely important feminist analysis of the Renaissance; the author answers her question with a resounding no.

Felix Gilbert, *Machiavelli and Guiccardini: Politics and History in Sixteenth Century Florence* (1984). Within the framework of the sociology of knowledge, both writers are placed in their political and intellectual context.

Myron Gilmore, *The World of Humanism* (1962). A thorough introduction to humanism in all its aspects.

J. R. Hale, *Renaissance Europe: The Individual and Society* (1978). Focuses on a feature of the Renaissance, individualism, that has been hotly debated.

CHAPTER TWELVE

Contacts with Non-Europeans Before Columbus

Though long a standard in most college history curricula, Western Civilization courses have recently been the target of criticism for a number of reasons. Given the increasingly pluralistic nature of American society, the argument goes, does it make any sense to require, or even recommend, that all students learn about the Western tradition and not about the Eastern tradition as well? Is not the notion of "civilization" itself, traditionally defined as the products of a small group of mostly upper-class males, elitist? If Western civilization is taught through standard texts, who selects these texts (often termed "Great Books")? Is there any way to make the canon more comprehensive while still emphasizing that cultural egalitarianism was never seen as a virtue until very recently? Instead of Western civilization, should we not all teach world civilization, like many of our colleagues? Many of us have doubts about why we are teaching the course, especially because the most vocal defenders of Western civilization as a subject often have a much narrower view of it than we do.

These debates have not been limited to scholarly journals and faculty meetings, but have reached the public press and television newsmagazines. They became particularly heated in 1992, the quincentenary of Columbus, as celebrations and anticelebrations focused on what is usually considered the first significant contact between Europeans and non-Europeans. In the first edition of this book, we also focused on the period of the earliest New World explorations, asking students to analyze European motivations for exploration and reactions to the New World. For this second edition, we have decided to change the focus, not to avoid the controversy over Columbus, but to let students explore his mental world more carefully by studying what he might have known about previous contacts between Europeans and non-Europeans. We hope this will both place Columbus more clearly within his historical context, as part of a long stream of medieval explorers, and lead students to consider why his voyages were extraordinary, why they changed the world more than those of his medieval predecessors.

The Problem

Content objectives:

1. to learn about medieval contacts between Europeans and non-Europeans

2. to learn how preconceptions might have shaped the initial contacts between Columbus and the natives of the New World

3. to examine the importance of religious factors among Columbus's motivations

Skills objectives:

1. to make distinctions between expectations and actual observations in written reports

2. to assess how authors' aims might have shaped their observations or reports

3. to trace the transformation of ideas over time, through direct influence and oral tradition

4. to identify letter-writing conventions

Though your students are no doubt very familiar with (and perhaps tired of) the story of Columbus, by setting him against his medieval predecessors this chapter provides a clear link between the Middle Ages and the modern world, something many of our students have difficulty seeing. It provides a historical perspective for some modern problems, and it could serve as the basis for a much broader discussion of Europe's relations with the rest of the world as well as the history of race relations. You may choose to return to this chapter later, when covering either nineteenth-century imperialism (Volume II, Chapter 9) or present-day relations between Europe and the wider world (Volume II, Chapter 15).

Though counterfactual discussions are often not very enlightening, in this case they might be. In fact, a number of articles have posited what the world might look like today had contacts between Europeans and non-Europeans developed differently. Once your students have analyzed the sources in this chapter, you may wish to pose questions such as these: How might relations between Europe and Asia have differed had the Mongol Empire not collapsed and travelers such as Marco Polo and Rabban Sauma increased in number? How might relations have been different had the Turks not taken Constantinople at a time when Europeans were technically able to carry out long ocean voyages such as those of the Portuguese and Columbus? Even more speculatively, how might Europe's relations with other continents have developed if Viking voyages to Newfoundland, or Portuguese fishing expeditions to the Newfoundland Grand Banks (which some historians now speculate preceded Columbus), had been more widely known?

Sources and Method

Very often junior high and high school history courses present the European expeditions to the New World in heroic terms as the first chapter of American history, with the explorers fueled by the same sort of idealistic drive for knowledge that later led to the U.S. space program. Some of the celebrations of the Columbus quincentenary drew parallels between sixteenth- and twentieth-century exploration even more strongly, viewing both in either a positive or a negative light. (The motivations of those instrumental in the space program, too, have come in for their share of debunking.) Both champions and critics of the "Age of Exploration" regard the voyages as an outgrowth of the rise of rationalism and secularism that began in the Renaissance and continued into the Scientific and Industrial Revolutions. Viewed in this light, the "Age of Exploration" fits conveniently into both the progressive model of U.S. or Western history and its critical revisionist version. The problem with this view is that it totally misrepresents, as we hope your students will discover in this chapter, the aims and motivations of the early explorers, subtracting them from the medieval context within which they operated.

In providing the background for this chapter, we have found it useful to review briefly the political history of central Asia, of which the highlights are mentioned in this section, for even students who have some background in European or Western history have no familiarity with Asian history. Under Genghis Khan (c. 1160–1227), the Mongols, one of many nomadic tribes in central Asia, expanded their holdings widely, taking Beijing in 1215 and most of northern China by the death of Genghis. Genghis was a brilliant military leader and effective ruler, as were many of his descendants. In the middle of the thirteenth century, the Mongols and their allies took Persia and Mesopotamia, overthrowing the caliph at Baghdad, and much of Russia, including Moscow and Kiev. Their conquests were brutal and ruthless, but once their hold was established, the Mongols encouraged trade and commerce. Genghis's grandson, Kublai Khan (1215?–1297), ruled the empire from 1260 until his death, promoting economic prosperity by rebuilding the Grand Canal, repairing public granaries, and extending highways. He supported scholarship and the arts, tolerated all religions (though he himself favored Buddhism), and opened his capital at Khanbalik (modern Beijing) to all visitors. In the 1260s, the Mongols attempted to take Syria, but they were unsuccessful, defeated by the Mameluke sultan of Egypt. The mission of Rabban Sauma, from which Source 2 derives, is a Mongol attempt to enlist European help in a new campaign against the Mamelukes in Syria, an attempt which came to nothing.

Source 3 derives from another perhaps missed opportunity for improved European-Mongol relations, this time in the area of religion. During the thirteenth century, many Mongols seem to have been interested in Christian ideas, and Kublai Khan asked the pope to send him missionaries. At that point, the popes were primarily involved in fighting with the Holy Roman emperors, so they never sent more than a few missionaries, of whom John of Monte Corvino was one. The Muslims were much more active during this period, converting many western Mongols, and the small Christian missionary effort ended completely when the Mongols were overthrown in 1368 and the antiforeign Ming dynasty came to power.

Maps are especially helpful in discussing European-Asian relations; it would be best if you could juxtapose ones of the Islamic caliphate in the eighth century, the Mongol Empire in the thirteenth, and the Turkish conquests of the sixteenth. If you have not yet discussed the cultural biases implicit in maps and geographical concepts, this would be an appropriate place to do so, because modern mapmaking began in the era of Columbus. Using any of the three maps noted above—maps that include both Europe and Asia—you might first ask your students their definition of a continent, and then ask them, given those criteria, why Europe is considered a continent and not simply western Asia. Using an older map of the world, which places Europe in the center and divides Asia in two, ask them what cultural presuppositions this reveals; then compare this with a newer map, with the east coast of the United States in the center. Medieval maps, with Jerusalem in the center, will help reinforce the point of this chapter about the religious world view of early explorers. Recent "alternative" world maps, which place the southern hemisphere on the top or adjust the scale so that the countries of the southern hemisphere appear with the correct size relative to those of the northern hemisphere, will address the issue of cultural bias in maps directly.

Along with a discussion of events in central Asia, we have found it useful in providing background for this chapter to review the Crusades and to summarize briefly the history of Spain up to the voyages of Columbus. It was no accident that Columbus was sponsored by Ferdinand and Isabella, nor that they finally agreed to his voyage in 1492 rather than earlier. Most of what became Spain was of course conquered by the Muslims in their initial drive of expansion, so medieval Spanish history is the story of the reconquest of the peninsula by Spanish armies. Spanish culture was thus dominated by knightly ideals for a much longer time than the rest of Europe; long after the Crusades had ended in Palestine and the Christian kingdoms there had faded to a memory, Spanish soldiers still thought of themselves as warriors in a crusade against the heathen. In actuality, as Christian holdings grew, many Muslims did not leave Spain; converting nominally to Christianity, they chose to stay in the Spanish villages or cities where their ancestors had lived for centuries. This was the same decision made by many Jews who had long lived under the tolerant Muslim overlordship. By the fifteenth century, then, large numbers of *conversos*, converted Muslims and Jews, and even some who had not converted, lived in many parts of Spain.

Until the reign of Ferdinand and Isabella, the *conversos* lived in relative harmony with their Christian neighbors. Those two rulers, whose marriage transformed Spain into a united kingdom for the first time, also wanted to achieve total homogeneity in Spanish culture. They conducted a successful military campaign against Granada, the last Muslim stronghold, finally conquering it in 1492. In the same year they expelled all practicing Jews and intensified the investigation and persecution of *conversos* suspected of maintaining their Jewish or Muslim beliefs. Simply having Jewish or Muslim ancestors was enough to make a person suspect, and all nobles and officials had to prove that their families had long been Christian, that their "blood was pure." (This notion of "purity of the blood" marked the first time in Europe that Jewishness was defined in racial rather than religious terms, that is, as an inheritable characteristic. Many historians see this policy of Ferdinand and Isabella as the beginning of modern-style anti-Semitism.)

Having driven the Muslims from Spanish soil, Ferdinand and Isabella were looking for other ways to continue their crusade and provide military employment for the class of knights and nobles who for generations had been fighting Muslims. Part of their drive for uniformity and centralized control involved diminishing the power of the nobility and increasing the dependence of nobles on the Crown. It was at this point that the pair finally agreed to support Columbus.

Columbus himself was just as inspired by crusading zeal as Ferdinand and Isabella, or perhaps more so. His deep religious convictions emerge in Source 1, and also in other of his writings. Columbus saw himself as appointed by God not only to spread Christianity but specifically to carry out a campaign against the Muslims. Even his given name he regarded as a sign from God, generally signing it "XP-fero," which roughly translates as "Christ carrier." (*XP* represents the first two letters of Christ's name in Greek, a standard symbol for Christ; *fero* is Latin for "I carry.") Your students may be skeptical about religious motives, viewing them as simply a pious means of veiling greed or racism; but given what we know about Columbus, such expressions seem to have been authentic.

The Evidence

Most of the sources in this chapter should be very easy for your students to understand because they were deliberately written or edited to appeal to a broad audience. Sources 4 and 5 in particular come from two of the most widely read medieval texts, and they were designed in some ways to be page-turners. You may have to provide a bit of assistance with the archaisms of Source 5, although we have provided footnotes for the words that might prove most problematic, and the other archaic turns of speech are repeated so often your students should become familiar with them.

For Sources 2 and 3, you may need to field specific questions about the structure of the medieval church, particularly the development of different religious orders and the duties and powers of the cardinals. Though the Nestorians are identified in footnote 25, you should probably be sure your students understand that they were not the only group that developed ideas different from the main bodies of the Eastern and Western churches; you could refer students back to the discussion of the development of orthodoxy within Christianity in Chapter 4.

Questions to Consider

This section asks students to read Source 1 yet a third time, to look for ideas and observations that do not appear to have been influenced by Columbus's preconceptions. Though the notion of reading something three times may make many students groan, this might be a good time to point out that that is exactly what historians, and particularly intellectual historians, do. Scholars of literature do the same, of course. Having students make the effort may help them see why some historians and literary scholars can spend their lives studying the texts of one writer, or sometimes a single text by one writer. The process may also help students understand how scholars can change their minds about the works they study, and how widely divergent opinions about certain texts may be held by different scholars.

This section also addresses the issue of letter-writing conventions, which provide another layer, along with intellectual preconceptions, that students must learn to strip away when using letters as historical documents. The section ends with questions that ask students to consider how explorers' preconceptions might have been reinforced by the actions of the people they met. Anthropologists and historians studying the explorations by Europeans in Africa have discovered a number of ways in which such reinforcement operated. For example, although it is doubtful that any Africans actually engaged in cannibalism, people would often report to explorers that those in the next village were cannibals; the explorers seemed to enjoy hearing this, and it was the worst thing people could think of to say about neighbors with whom they might have been fighting for generations. Scholars have also discovered that Christian hymns were passed between villages in advance of the explorers, because the singing of hymns was an easy way to please the Europeans; this fueled the mistaken idea that a Christian kingdom like Prester John's existed somewhere in Africa. Thus, Columbus's comments that the natives he encountered reported gold, cannibals, and people with tails on other islands may very well reflect what he was actually told. Caribbean cultural conventions may have taught that one should always humor strangers who have odd ideas.

Epilogue and Evaluation

We hope this chapter will stimulate your students to reflect on their own cultural biases as well as on the ways in which European cultural prejudices have shaped the history of the world. The best means of evaluation might be a reflective essay. For in-class activities and opportunities for evaluation, a debate centered on some of the counterfactual questions posed above might be fun, with students assigned to represent various viewpoints, such as that of a central Asian bureaucrat, an Italian Church official, a Portuguese explorer, a Viking leader, and a West African tribal chieftain. Playing roles such as these will encourage students to think about cultural biases not only of Europeans, but also of residents of other parts of the world, and the debate may move beyond mere speculation.

For Further Reading

Daniel J. Boorstin, *The Discoverers: A History of Man's Search to Know His World and Himself* (1985). A wide-ranging and erudite discussion, written for a popular audience, of human discoveries in geography, biology, and human nature from Sumerian times to the present.

Mary B. Campbell, *The Witness and the Other World: Exotic European Travel Writing 400–1600* (1988). A fascinating analysis of over a millennium of European confrontations with "the other" and the geographic and cultural notions that arose from these.

Valerie I. J. Flint, *The Imaginative Landscape of Christopher Columbus* (1992). A new work that focuses on how Columbus's notions influenced his reports on his discoveries.

Jacques Gernet, *China and the Christian Impact: A Conflict of Cultures*, trans. Janet Lloyd (1985). Explores early Chinese reactions to Christianity, from the first contacts with missionaries to the seventeenth century.

Samuel Eliot Morison, *Christopher Columbus: Admiral of the Ocean Sea* (1953). Still the best standard biography, by one of the premier American historians.

Boise Penrose, *Travel and Discovery in the Renaissance 1420–1620* (1952). A good survey, which also discusses travelers before the Portuguese explorations.

J. R. S. Phillips, *The Medieval Expansion of Europe* (1988). Looks at the relations between Europe and Asia, Africa, and America before Columbus: how these shaped medieval popular and scholarly understanding and influenced the Age of Exploration.

CHAPTER THIRTEEN

The Spread of the Reformation (also Volume II, Chapter 1)

In assigning a name to our own age, some scholars prefer "the postindustrial period" and others call it "the Communications Age." Given the virtually worldwide spread of telephones and televisions—and more recently of copiers, fax machines, and home computers—the latter is an apt title. With instantaneous communication between different parts of the globe now possible, the barriers to communication today are political rather than technological.

The present revolution in communications is not the first ever experienced in Western history, however; actually it is the third. The first was the invention of writing in ancient Mesopotamia, and the second was that explored here: the invention of the printing press with movable metal type. In both of these eras, as well as in our own, new methods of communication did not replace older ones but rather augmented them, making available a greater range of methods to those with information or ideas to disseminate. The resulting "multimedia campaign" made the ideas themselves appear more powerful simply because people heard, saw, and read the same information many times. As Marshall McLuhan and others have made us realize, the way in which ideas are communicated shapes both the ideas themselves and how people come to understand them.

Martin Luther's reformation was a successful media campaign not only because of the methods he employed but also because many groups in German society found parts of his message extremely attractive. He was able to give voice to religious, social, and political grievances that had been sporadically expressed for years, leading diverse groups to adopt him as their champion. Some of this broad-based support resulted either from a misperception or from a deliberately selective interpretation of what Luther actually said. Though Luther did not consciously attempt to provide something for everyone, this is in fact what he accomplished, thereby setting a pattern for later religious and political propaganda campaigns. Modern-day political advertising consultants know that catering to the interests of every social group is the best way to make a candidate and his or her ideas appealing. With their catchy slogans, vilification of opponents, musical ditties, and repetition of easily understood concepts, modern political advertising campaigns are the direct descendants of the Protestant Reformation, though Luther himself would no doubt be horrified at the thought. Our own communications revolution may be increasing the speed at which information is spread, but the sixteenth-century communications revolution was the first to produce a dramatic increase in the size of the audience, creating the "media markets" that advertisers and political leaders alike now court so assiduously.

The Problem

Content objectives:

1. to understand Martin Luther's key theological ideas

2. to examine the various means by which these ideas were spread

3. to learn how various groups within German society interpreted these ideas

4. to learn about the economic, social, and political background of the religious movement we call the Reformation

Skills objectives:

1. to assess the symbolic content of visual evidence

2. to read songs, hymns, or plays for their ideological content

3. to compare the ideas communicated through different types of evidence

Besides these specific objectives, this chapter lends itself to a broader discussion of the way in which various ideas have been successfully or unsuccessfully communicated throughout history. For an even more far-ranging debate, you might discuss the shaping of people's views of the world by the means they use to receive information. The latter idea has been most widely popularized by Marshall McLuhan (especially in *The Global Village* and *The Medium Is the Message*), but Walter Ong's thoughts on the subject are more stimulating and thought provoking, especially his conclusions about the relations between religious change and changes in means of communication. In *The Presence of the Word*, Ong notes that the two major changes in the Judeo-Christian tradition, the birth of Christ and the Protestant Reformation, both occurred at periods in which the basic means of communication was changing: the birth of Christ at the time when written information was becoming more important than oral, and the Protestant Reformation at the time when handwritten manuscripts gave way to print. For Ong, it is not simply the new methods but the *simultaneous* presence of older and newer methods that explains why first Christianity and then Protestantism spread so rapidly; both religions used traditional channels while also developing their own, newer methods of communication. Ong also points out the special importance attached to the "word" in Christianity (Christ himself is defined in this way in the Gospel of John); in no other religion does "spreading the word" take on quite the same significance, literal as well as symbolic.

Though *The Presence of the Word*, as well as Ong's subsequent *The Interstices of the Word*, would probably be difficult for many of your students, we recommend both works, especially the former, as references for the philosophical implications of alterations in methods of spreading and receiving information (what Ong terms "changes in the sensorium.") A teaser question for your class: What is the difference between an oral culture's perception of a word, as existing in time, and a manuscript/print culture's perception of the same word as it exists in space? In cultures of the first sort, a word disappears after the sound is uttered; in cultures of the latter type, the word can be returned to again and again. Other differences can be identified as well. Such questions, which may seem to stray from the subject of this chapter, in reality do not. Protestantism put great emphasis on the written word and the individual's access to that word, whereas Catholicism held that most believers should merely hear the word and only the elite should actually see or read it.

Another, somewhat less nebulous topic suggested by this chapter is the role of literacy. Though there is great dispute about literacy rates in Renaissance and early modern Europe, most researchers agree that they rose significantly and that this increase in literacy both contributed to and partially resulted from the spread of the Protestant Reformation. You may wish to open a discussion on this issue by asking your students to imagine what society would be like if the majority of the population could not read or at least have contact with someone who read. Has the role of literacy in our society diminished with the advent of television and the return to an oral sensorium for many people?

Sources and Method

The first question in this chapter asks students to assess how Luther's ideas were spread; they should be able to draw their answers from the sources with no additional background. The second question—how these ideas were made attractive to various groups—may require some additional background about the economic, political, and social situation in sixteenth-century Germany. This frame also makes it possible to explore the reasons Luther's ideas carried so much greater impact than those of Wyclif, Hus, and other medieval reformers, even though the content of their ideas was not radically different. It is important, however, not to let secular background factors make students forget that the Reformation was initially (and, in terms of Luther's involvement, always) a religious movement.

In terms of method, we have advised students to pay attention to both ideas and images and to make a list of those they find frequently repeated. We have also suggested that they note negative ideas and images, those that criticize the Catholic church or an existing situation, and positive ideas and images, those that are innovative or put greater emphasis on certain aspects of Christianity. The sophistication of your students will determine whether they need some assistance in this process. You will want to make especially sure that they include Luther's most important ideas—particularly his emphases on faith alone, grace alone, and Scripture alone—and his criticisms of reason, of philosophy, and of relying on good works for salvation. These key ideas come out most clearly in the sermon (Source 1) and in Speratus's hymn (Source 4).

The hymn also tackles the problematic question of the role played by an individual's actions if salvation is totally dependent on God's free gift of grace. We have discovered that this is often the first question students raise when they discuss Luther's or Calvin's theology: if getting into heaven is God's decision, why be good? Verses 3 and 4 of the hymn present what will become the standard Lutheran answer, that the Law (by which Luther and his followers meant the requirements set by God in the Old Testament) was fulfilled for all people by Christ, but that if one has true faith one will freely want to do good things—or, as the hymn succinctly puts it, "By its fruits true faith is known." Luther himself made this point in many of his later sermons, when the social upheavals of the Peasants' War and the more radical ideas of many other reformers led him to place ever greater emphasis on obedience to authority; again and again he stressed that the "freedom" Christ had brought to those with true faith was totally spiritual. The sermon reprinted in this chapter is a very early one from Luther's most radical period, but we have chosen it rather than a later, more typically conservative effort to allow students to discover just how revolutionary Luther's initial sermons were and to see why so many groups could interpret them as a call to arms. (You may also point out, however, that the seeds of his later conservatism were already present, particularly in the statement, "When persons are servants or maidservants, their work should benefit their master.")

The Evidence

Rather than using excerpts, we have reprinted the entire sermon as Source 1 to give students the full flavor of Luther's language and allow them to follow his line of argument. You may wish to comment that this was a relatively short sermon by sixteenth-century standards; both Catholic and Protestant preachers could orate at great length, and later Protestant services were often several hours in length. (This tradition continued in Puritan New England, where the devout were often required to spend five or six hours in church on Sundays. The sermons of Jonathan Edwards often lasted well over an hour.) Luther's two hymns (Sources 2 and 3) have been included primarily to convey a sense of his style as well as of his exhortations to believers to depend completely on God for their salvation. The strongly martial flavor of the hymns often obscured this emphasis, however, for at certain points they also seem to be encouraging the believer to fight for the true religion: "Let this world's tyrant rage/In battle we'll engage."

We have provided fairly extensive clues to help students understand the content and symbolism of the woodcuts (Sources 5 through 9). Most depict only negative images, because it was much easier, and more titillating, to portray the wrongs of the Catholic church than what was right about Protestant ideas; Source 5 is the only one containing any positive imagery. The negative portrayals also drew on a long tradition of criticism of the Church; artists knew people were accustomed to seeing monks portrayed as wolves or the pope as an avid money collector. In contrast, the symbols that expressed the new Protestant theology had to be created fresh, and people had to be instructed in what they represented. To understand the positive imagery of Source 5, for example, one would have to know that Luther kept baptism and communion as sacraments, a fact of which not everyone who saw this woodcut would have been aware. The bluntness of Source 9 (the two men defecating into the papal tiara) may offend some of your students, but ideas were commonly expressed in crass and vulgar terms in the sixteenth century. Luther himself (to say nothing of Rabelais) often talked about shitting and farting (his language), and his comments on the Roman clergy became increasingly scatological as he grew older.

The dialogue (Source 10), like many of Luther's sermons and treatises, first appeared as a pamphlet. Scholars have just begun to study the thousands of Reformation pamphlets that appeared during the sixteenth century, and several historians at the University of Tübingen are creating a computerized inventory of all surviving pamphlets from this period. Because they were printed on cheap paper without permanent covers and often in small editions, many have simply disappeared. Despite their seemingly ephemeral nature, the pamphlets provide a good means of tracing the ways in which ideas were spread to ordinary people; they were cheap enough for large numbers of people to buy. As this example indicates, common people were convinced that the Last Judgment was imminent; many viewed the attacks of the Turks and the problems of the Church as signs that the end of the world was near.

Questions to Consider

In this section, students are asked first to weigh the effects of printed as opposed to oral means of transmitting the message of the Reformation. When you discuss the revolutionary effects of the printing press, you may wish to emphasize that it made possible the wide dissemination not only of texts but of pictures and hymns as well. For the first time certain artists, including many such as Dürer who accepted and promoted Reformation ideas, were able to enjoy a reputation throughout western Europe. Their woodcuts, often printed with a line or two of text, helped people learn how to read in the same way that children use illustrated readers today. Of course, the person who learned Luther's message primarily through visual images and simple text would not have grasped his more complex theological points and may have viewed the Reformation as a more negative than positive movement. We must not assume, however, that illiterate or newly literate people were not able to understand complex points of theology. As we saw in Chapter 10 of Volume I, common people could develop elaborate religious ideas independently of university-trained theologians, could explain Christianity in sophisticated terms, and could choose to accept certain parts of Christianity and reject others.

The second part of this section asks students to distinguish among social groups in analyzing the communication of the Protestant message. It will probably be easiest for your students to see how Reformation ideas were made attractive to peasants and poor people, because the sources contain overt criticism of Church and secular leaders and portray common people sympathetically. You should note again that these sources all come from the earliest years of the Reformation, when Luther and others viewed the "common man" as the ultimate savior of Germany. After the Peasants' War, negative portrayals of peasants as stupid, oafish, or devious were much more common. None of the sources reprinted here come from peasants themselves, of course, so we must be somewhat tentative in judging how the positive portrayal of common people was actually interpreted.

Epilogue and Evaluation

The epilogue has two parts, the first a brief summary of the results of Lutheran propaganda of the sort reprinted here, and the second a discussion of some of the further repercussions of printing. Hand in hand with printing came censorship as religious and political authorities attempted to control people's access to the ideas now spread so widely and rapidly by printed materials. Early modern attempts at censorship were never very successful, and authorities gradually realized it was easier to control people's opinions by providing their own propaganda than by attempting to ban alternative ideas.

To evaluate this chapter, you may wish to ask students to collect current examples of the various ways in which religious leaders communicate their ideas. This assignment can lead to a consideration of the differences between the communications revolution of the twentieth century and that which took place in the sixteenth century. The second question could also serve as the basis for wider research projects in which students explore the political, social, religious, and economic grievances of sixteenth-century Germany in greater depth.

For Further Reading

Peter Burke, *Popular Culture in Early Modern Europe* (1978). Examines the ways in which religious and other ideas were transmitted to and by common people, and the interplay between popular and elite culture. Burke views the early modern period as a time that witnessed the suppression of popular culture.

Carl Christensen, *Art and the Reformation in Germany* (1981). Explores both Protestantism's iconoclasm and its use and support of art; in contrast to earlier studies, sees the Reformation as generally beneficial to artistic production.

Elizabeth Eisenstein, *The Printing Press as an Agent of Change* (1979). A monumental study of the impact of the printing press in all aspects of culture.

Robert W. Scribner, *For the Sake of Simple Folk: Popular Propaganda for the German Reformation* (1981). An extremely innovative analysis of the means by which the Lutheran message was spread to the common people, with numerous woodcuts and engravings.

Gerald Strauss, *Luther's House of Learning: The Indoctrination of the Young in the German Reformation* (1978). A highly controversial study, which argues that the Reformation was ultimately unsuccessful in its attempts to transmit religious knowledge and change popular behavior.

CHAPTER FOURTEEN

Staging Absolutism (also Volume II, Chapter 2)

King of France for almost three-quarters of a century, Louis XIV has long fascinated historians because his reign marked the culmination of those trends in government traditionally called "absolute monarchy." Professional historians have focused their attention on the ideological and institutional aspects of this monarch's state building. We have found that students, however, are more drawn to the individual who, as king, consciously created a role and setting for himself designed to enhance royal power. Our purpose in this chapter is to connect the institutional and personal elements of Louis XIV's long reign as a way of helping students understand the process by which the absolute monarchy was created in seventeenth- and eighteenth-century Europe.

The Problem

Content objectives:

1. to understand the theoretical basis of royal absolutism

2. to understand the ways in which court etiquette and ceremony were designed to reflect and embody the king's authority

3. to identify the symbols of royal power in the palace of Versailles

Skills objectives:

1. to analyze written works of political theory

2. to visualize the past through memoir literature while understanding the uses and limitations of this medium

3. to examine visual evidence and to understand the political purposes that sometimes underlie artists' and architects' work

4. to combine visual and written evidence in analyzing a historical problem

As with all the chapters in this book, this chapter can be used as the foundation for discussion of broader issues in your course. The following are a few possibilities:

1. What were the problems of political authority in the late medieval and early modern periods?

2. Is the maintenance of order and security in a society compatible with individual freedom? You may wish students particularly to reread Source 1, the selection by Jean Bodin, as a basis for this discussion. You may also wish to introduce the thought of Thomas Hobbes, whose *Leviathan* (1651) expresses the need for strong political authority as the only alternative to anarchy.

3. Is Louis XIV's use of the Versailles palace and its court ceremony symptomatic of trends in Western politics through the present day that seem to place greater emphasis on form over substance? Did Louis XIV himself actually possess the real-world power to match the symbols?

You may, of course, wish students to address a broad question that you may have raised in an introductory lecture. This chapter provides a plentiful supply of discussion topics because it presents both the theoretical basis for absolutism and the symbolic means by which this political theory was advanced.

Sources and Method

Students are faced in this chapter with the challenging goal of combining political theory with its written and visual expression. You may wish to facilitate the learning process by a discussion that reinforces the general significance of the kinds of sources the chapter offers.

The first questions address the theoretical foundations of absolutism. A general discussion of some of the major works of Western political theory through the seventeenth century might be worthwhile as an introduction to these questions. Students should be prompted to recognize that the writings of Bodin and Bossuet belong to a body of works, including Marsilius of Padua's *Defender of the Peace* (1324), Machiavelli's *The Prince* (1532), and Thomas Hobbes's *Leviathan*, that helped to define political life in the early modern period. All these works reflected the historical experience of their respective periods, and you may wish to reinforce the link the chapter makes between the political theories of Bodin and Bossuet and their active participation in the politics of their age.

The chapter guides students in drawing out basic ideas from these two political thinkers but then asks them to identify evidence of these ideas in court ceremony, art, and architecture. As we point out in the chapter, an understanding of political symbolism is of fundamental importance to the members of any political system. Court ceremony, presented in the *Memoirs* of Saint-Simon, is the first expression of such symbolism represented in this chapter. You may wish to use this selection as the starting point for a more basic discussion of the role of the European nobility. You may wish to pose such questions as: What had that role been in the medieval period? Judging by Bodin's thinking, what had it become in the seventeenth century?

The art and architecture of Versailles create an image of the king's status and prestige. You may wish to add to the chapter's pictorial evidence other examples of the symbols of royal power that confronted seventeenth-century French people, such as music, the royal coronation ceremony, and the persistence of beliefs in the sacred and magical power of kingship. Basic sources for this discussion may be found at the end of this chapter.

The Evidence

Students are using several kinds of evidence in this chapter, and you may wish to reinforce their understanding of the different analytical methods they should employ. Sources 1 and 2 are political treatises from which students are expected to derive the authors' concepts of royal sovereignty. Bodin's treatise is relatively easy reading. The second work, by Bossuet, may prove more challenging to students. In the Sources and Method section of the text, we have already pointed out Bossuet's status as a cleric and his use of political sources to justify his political thought. You may wish to emphasize these points again to guide students in reading his work; it may also be helpful to note that Bossuet derived his format from medieval Scholastic traditions for developing an argument.

Source 3 should be easy and fairly enjoyable reading for students. They will be guided by our questions to understand the symbolism of the court ceremony Saint-Simon describes, but you may also wish to emphasize the selection as a lesson in understanding sources. What point of view does Saint-Simon betray in his *Memoirs*?

In Sources 4 through 13, we run the risk that students will give only cursory attention to pictorial evidence. The questions in this chapter encourage careful study of the pictures as expressions of ideology, and you may wish to reinforce that analytical approach to art by citing modern examples of symbolic art and architecture. You might start students thinking along these lines by asking some of the following questions: What message about democracy and American society is found in the murals decorating the post offices built in many of our communities by the Works Progress Administration during the 1930s? Why does much of the public architecture of Washington, D.C., or any state capital attempt to recreate elements of Greek and Roman architecture?

Questions to Consider

In every chapter this section poses general questions that should guide students in combining the answers to leading questions posed in Sources and Method with the results of their own analysis for an understanding of the general problem of the chapter. In this chapter, because the intellectual jump from understanding political theory to discerning its expression is a rather sophisticated one, you may especially want to guide students with a discussion of the classical and biblical sources for some of the pictorial evidence they have examined. You may wish to explore with them the reasons for the predominance of biblical and classical forms in the art, architecture, and some of the ceremonies such as the Carousel of 1662.

Epilogue and Evaluation

The purpose of the epilogue is to take students beyond France and the reign of Louis XIV into the wider framework of Western history. You may wish to use this occasion as the jumping-off point for a lecture on absolutism and its influence on political development in western European countries. You may wish to pose questions on the role of state building by Louis XIV and other monarchs of his age in the creation of the modern state. You may also wish to expand on the chapter by exploring the work of Frederick William the Great Elector in Prussia, Tsar Peter the Great of Russia, and Emperor Leopold I of Austria.

The epilogue also lends itself to a potentially fascinating visual essay that instructors may wish to mount with slides available in many of the Western Civilization slide collections currently on the market. A discussion of the use of political symbols could range from the Age of Absolutism through such twentieth-century political symbols as Nazi regalia (discussed in Chapter 13 of Volume II) as well as the use of the American flag as a backdrop for U.S. presidential candidates.

Several options are open to the instructor in evaluating student mastery of the chapter. Classroom discussion of the symbolic expression of political theory can be highly productive and may even include oral analysis of some of the visual evidence. The debate format is also a useful mode of evaluation, as is role playing. Saint-Simon's memoirs present the observations of a man essentially critical of the curbs on noble independence and power created by the monarchy, whereas Bodin provides arguments for enhanced royal authority in the name of order and security. In a role-playing situation some students could assume the role of French noblemen resentful of their loss of autonomy in Versailles court life and an absolutist state; they would argue for their historic freedoms as one-time knightly defenders of the state. Other role players, as ministers of the king, might respond with the religious justification for royal power and, more important, the necessity of such power because of the religious civil warfare that divided sixteenth-century France.

Written assignments could ask students to weave material from textbook and lectures together with the contents of this chapter in a variety of essay topics. You could ask them, for example, to examine the obstacles to strong central government in early modern Europe and to explore the abstract theory and real-world practices by which monarchs overcame those impediments.

For Further Reading

J. W. Allen, *A History of Political Thought in the Sixteenth Century* (1928). An old but still basic work, especially concise on Bodin.

William Beik, *Absolutism in Seventeenth-Century France: State Power and Provincial Aristocracy in Languedoc* (1985). An important study of the local impact of absolutism, emphasizing that Louis XIV's government represented the final perfection of feudal institutions of government.

Marc Bloch, *The Royal Touch: Sacred Monarchy and Scrofula in England and France*, trans. J. E. Anderson (1973). A study of the mystical aspects of medieval kingship by one of France's greatest historians.

Julian H. Franklin, *Jean Bodin and the Rise of Absolutist Theory* (1973). A modern study of Bodin's thought.

Pierre Goubert, *Louis XIV and Twenty Million Frenchmen*, trans. Anne Carter (1970). A history of Louis's reign from the perspective of his subjects, by a master of French social history.

Robert W. Hartle, "The Allegory of Versailles: Then and Now," *Laurels* 52 (1981): 9–18. A study of the symbolism of the palace. See also the same author's excellent essay, "Louis XIV and the Mirror of Antiquity," in *The Sun King: Louis XIV and the New World*, ed. Steven G. Reinhardt and Vaughn L. Glasgow (1984).

Christopher Hibbert, *Versailles* (1972). A well-illustrated history of the palace.

Robert Isherwood, *Music in the Service of the King: France in the Seventeenth Century* (1973). A study of the use of music to enhance the image of absolutism.

Richard A. Jackson, *Vive le Roi! A History of the French Coronation Ceremony from Charles V to Charles X* (1984). A study of the royal coronation ceremony and its meaning.

Roland E. Mousnier, *The Institutions of France Under the Absolute Monarchy, 1598–1789*, 2 vols., trans. Brian Pierce and Arthur Goldhammer (1979, 1984). A comprehensive study by one of the finest scholars of seventeenth-century France.

Armand Jean du Plessis, Duc de Richelieu, *The Political Testament of Cardinal Richelieu*, ed. and trans. Henry Bertram Hill (1968). A readable statement of goals and methods by one of the architects of French absolutism.

Guy Walton, *Louis XIV's Versailles* (1985). A profusely illustrated study of the palace by an art historian.

John B. Wolf, *Louis XIV* (1968). The best modern biography of the king in English.

CHAPTER THREE

The Mind of an Age: Science and Religion Confront Eighteenth-Century Natural Disaster

The Enlightenment was a crucial event in the intellectual history of the West. The thought of that period continues to influence Western societies in numerous ways, not the least of which is its political expression in the Constitution of the United States. We have found, however, that many students experience difficulty in understanding the abstract ideas of the Enlightenment. "Natural law" and the eighteenth-century quest to uncover it have little meaning for many of them. Students do follow current world events, however, and the press and the electronic media confront them with the daily spectacle of natural disasters around the world. By focusing on a single cataclysmic event, the Lisbon earthquake of 1755, and the reaction it provoked among European thinkers, this chapter provides modern students entry into one important aspect of Enlightenment thought: its explanation of the physical world. Students first confront traditional, theocentric explanations of the disaster. Then, as they read the chapter, students should be able to identify the roots of the Enlightenment in the Scientific Revolution, the Deistic outlook, and the genesis of doubt about divine efficacy as eighteenth-century observers gained a deeper understanding of the physical world around them.

The Problem

Content objectives:

1. to understand the traditional theological explanations of physical phenomena advanced by Western thinkers since the beginning of their civilization

2. to understand the intellectual revolution made possible by the theories of Newton and other figures of the Scientific Revolution

3. to understand Deism

4. to perceive the ultimate implications of the new scientific thought for traditional religion

Skills objectives:

1. to read religious and philosophical sources for the wealth of historical information they offer

2. to use the information from those sources to make general conclusions about the development of thought during a single historical epoch

As with previous chapters, this chapter's subject can be used to stimulate thought and discussion on a number of historical and present-day issues, including the following questions:

1. What ideas and attitudes presented in the selections do you find influential in modern thought?

2. What effect might the growing secularism evident in the later selections have had on the respect accorded the Church and, indeed, on other traditional institutions by the late eighteenth century?

Sources and Method

The selections in this chapter are brief, but taken together they present significant challenges to students. Some of the vocabulary is distinctly antiquated, and the texts abound in biblical and other allusions with which students may have little familiarity. We have glossed such words and phrases in extensive footnotes. Texts such as these present other difficulties for student comprehension, however. Each expresses an aspect of Western thought, and the selections are arranged to present the progression of that thought during the eighteenth century. To aid students in understanding the viewpoints expressed in the selections, we have provided an unusually lengthy introduction in our Problem and Sources and Method sections. You may wish to reinforce the message of those sections by further amplifying our background material on the Enlightenment. Certainly you will wish to encourage students to read critically and to understand the chronological development in thought taking place in the course of these selections.

This is the first chapter devoted to traditional intellectual history in Volume II of *Discovering the Western Past*. If you are using the book for the first time, you should note that the intellectual history chapters were developed as a group designed to present progressively more challenging interpretive problems to students. Therefore, you may decide to place special emphasis on skills development in this chapter. We have done this in our classes by assigning students in pairs to read a selection, analyze it jointly, and then make a brief oral report on its central idea and significance.

The Evidence

We have arranged this chapter's evidence to facilitate students' responses to the chapter's central questions. Those questions require that students identify the viewpoint in each selection, relate it to the immediate event of the earthquake, and place the author's views in the context of general Western intellectual development. This is a challenging task and one that may require your guidance.

For Sources 1 and 2 you may recall for students the importance of Christian theology in understanding Western sensibility during the medieval and early modern periods. With this background, students should find the outlook of Malagrida and Wesley more understandable.

Newtonian physics is a complex subject, and Voltaire's synopsis of Newton's basic ideas was included here instead of writings by Newton himself simply because Voltaire's popularization described the English scientist's basic work more clearly than Newton did himself. Nevertheless, you may wish to provide greater background on the Scientific Revolution to further clarify the significance of Newton's discoveries. The works of Johannes Kepler, Galileo, and others also contributed to the Enlightenment's vision of a world machine running according to mathematical laws.

Source 4 may prove especially difficult for students to interpret because it is a poem. Many students tend to dismiss poetry as incomprehensible and skip over it. It is important for them not to skip this poem, however, because Pope's message is essential: that God's physical laws will inevitably produce the greatest possible good for mankind. Thus, students must be encouraged to read the poem carefully, not only for its message, but to begin to develop the interpretive skills they will need for the poetry that appears in subsequent chapters.

Sources 5 and 6 present aspects of the scientific method. Again, students may need some encouragement to grasp fully the meaning of these selections. Source 5 on "observation" runs the risk of being dismissed by twentieth-century students as something to take for granted. They should be prompted to understand the intellectually revolutionary import of a scientific method of observation by recalling the theological explanations of physical phenomena given by Malagrida and Wesley. The Buffon selection may at first seem like fantasy to the students. They need to be reminded of the novelty of the search for a rational explanation of physical phenomena during this era.

Sources 7 and 8, both fairly straightforward, reflect the immediate debate on the earthquake's significance. Students may need some encouragement to draw the full meaning from Voltaire's poem.

Sources 9 and 10 by Hume and Baron d'Holbach should be carefully presented in the context of their age. These remarkable negations of traditional thought are clear expressions of the ultimate implications of the Enlightenment. When students are encouraged to contrast Sources 9 and 10 with Sources 1 and 2, the enormous impact of the Enlightenment should be apparent to them.

Questions to Consider

These questions have been formulated to guide students in analyzing the chapter's material. You may also wish to pose other questions in class discussion, but students will need your guidance in formulating their answers.

You may want to ask students to estimate the impact of Enlightenment ideas on eighteenth-century society. You may refer them, as a start, to the literacy figures provided in the next chapter of this manual. Those figures and other data constitute the starting point for what one of the authors regards as an essential discussion on the Enlightenment: to demonstrate that the thought of the *philosophes,* no matter how important, was not the thought of all western Europeans of that time. Many people were illiterate and thus ignorant of the *philosophes'* ideas. Robert Darnton, for example, in *The Business of Enlightenment: A Publishing History of the Encyclopedia, 1775–1800* (1979), has brought precision to our understanding of the impact of this great work.

Students also are fascinated by the persistence of a nonelite culture alongside that of the Enlightenment thinkers. Superstition, not the search for reason, dominated peasant minds: in eastern Europe, witch burning occurred as late as the 1790s. In the For Further Reading section, we offer several works that introduce popular culture.

Epilogue and Evaluation

The purpose of this chapter is to use natural disasters like the Lisbon earthquake as entry points for students into Enlightenment thought. Students should gain from the chapter a good general idea of the underlying concepts of the Enlightenment and the way in which the *philosophes* viewed the physical world around them.

The epilogue provides the basis for applying students' understanding of the Enlightenment to other spheres. This can be the starting point for a discussion of Enlightenment thought on government (Montesquieu, Rousseau, and others), criminal justice (Becarria), and economic life (French physiocrats like Quesnay and the Scotsman Adam Smith). The epilogue also provides a natural opening for a discussion of the so-called Enlightened Despots of the eighteenth century. The essential problem in studying these monarchs lies in the nature of the goals underlying the reforms of Pombal, Frederick the Great, Joseph II, Catherine the Great, and others. Did they adopt the cause of reform to gain an improved life for their subjects or enhanced power and revenue for themselves?

Evaluating student mastery of this chapter can take several forms. The central question—why the Lisbon earthquake posed such an intellectual crisis for eighteenth-century thinkers—might form the basis for a written assignment or an essay question. You may also wish to extend the scope of the chapter into the past and the future alike by asking students to discuss what the Western world view might have been had the Scientific Revolution and the Enlightenment not occurred.

For Further Reading

Peter Burke, *Popular Culture in Early Modern Europe* (1978). A stimulating essay on the culture of Europe's nonelites.

Herbert Butterfield, *The Origins of Modern Science, 1300–1800* (1957). A highly readable study of the Scientific Revolution and its intellectual impact.

William Doyle, *The Old European Order, 1660–1800* (1978). An excellent modern synthesis of recent scholarship on the population, economy, society, and government of eighteenth-century Europe. Written, like most histories of this period, with the French Revolution in view, it is a useful work for background on the period.

Peter Gay, *The Enlightenment: An Interpretation*, 2 vols. (1966, 1969). A detailed modern study of the Enlightenment.

Paul Hazard, *The European Mind, 1680–1715*, trans. J. Lewis May (1963). Now an old work, but still fundamental in understanding the intellectual implications of the new science. The French title translates as "The Crisis of the European Conscience," indicating the age's conflict between traditional religion and the new science. This work is complemented by its sequel, *European Thought in the Eighteenth Century from Montesquieu to Lessing*, trans. J. Lewis May (1963).

T. D. Kendrick, *The Lisbon Earthquake* (1957). A modern study of the earthquake and its intellectual ramifications.

Thomas S. Kuhn, *The Structure of Scientific Revolutions* (1962). A key work on the evolution of scientific thought.

Robert Muchembled, *Popular Culture and Elite Culture in France, 1400–1750*, trans. Lydia Cochrane (1985). A skilled social historian's study of popular culture in early modern France, offering an interpretation strikingly different from that of Burke.

Robert R. Palmer, *Catholics and Unbelievers in Eighteenth Century France* (1939). A study of those opposed to the Enlightenment.

Dale Van Kley, *The Jansenists and the Expulsion of the Jesuits from France, 1757–1765* (1975). An excellent modern study of the Jesuits and their expulsion from one Catholic country.

CHAPTER FOUR

A Statistical View of European Rural Life, 1600-1800

The preceding chapter presented students with a traditional but challenging approach to the past, a problem in intellectual history. Chapter 4 offers students a very different vision of the past in the findings of scholars practicing the relatively newer methods of social history. In its own way, social history can be as difficult a subject to present as the sometimes abstract concepts of intellectual history.

One problem in teaching social history stems from the attitudes students bring to the study of history in general. Despite the research of several generations of their teachers in the social history of Europe, today's students still enter the classroom expecting a history defined by great events. Indeed, they seem to be searching for the *histoire événementale* found so inadequate by Marc Bloch and Lucien Febvre, the two French pioneers in the methods of modern social history and founders of the journal *Annales: Economies, Sociétés, Civilisations*. Some students are disappointed when they find the "great event, great man" focus absent from their courses. In this chapter, we hope to spark their interest in other approaches to the past.

Another problem is that scholars often express the results of their research in this field in quantitative terms. We have noted among many of our students an aversion to numbers and quantitative analysis remarkable in this age in which the modern media constantly bombard us with statistical data. Because the trend toward statistical analysis can be expected only to intensify, not simply in the field of history but in our society at large, we have chosen to place major emphasis on the quantitative analysis of early modern European society by devoting this entire chapter to statistical sources. Our hope is not only to render numbers more comprehensible to students but also to invite them to understand the world of the illiterate majority of seventeenth- and eighteenth-century Europe, a world far different from that of the societal elites who produced the abstract ideas students analyzed in Chapter 3.

The Problem

Content objectives:

1. to understand the cultural level of the majority of early modern Europeans

2. to learn about the dietary consequences of a primitive agriculture

3. to understand the impact that the failure of such agriculture and the incidence of disease could have on a population

4. to understand the methods of social historians in such relatively new fields as the history of climate

Skills objectives:

1. to assemble quantitative data from the various forms of its expression: maps, simple and complex tables, and graphs

2. to draw conclusions from statistical information

3. to compare several kinds of statistics and to draw conclusions and patterns from that comparison

Sources and Method

This chapter, more than many others, brings students close to the real archival resources of history, and we have found that they have a great interest in the mechanics of historical research. One of the authors initiates class discussion by passing around photocopies of eighteenth-century manuscripts to illustrate the methods (and problems) of research in the history of an age whose population was largely illiterate and whose literate minority possessed neither typewriters nor word processors.

You may wish to open the class with a methodological discussion in which you point out the relative absence, for most of the population, of such traditional raw materials for historical research as letters, diaries, and so forth. Historians have been obliged to reconstruct the past of Europe's illiterate majority indirectly, through those few written sources, maintained by their social superiors, in which they left a record of their passage through life. In the process of discussing sources, students will learn more about early modern life.

Clergymen, judges, notaries, and policemen all left historians essential records on the illiterate majority of Europe's population. Clergymen kept records of baptisms, marriages, and burials; especially in Catholic countries where the Council of Trent mandated such records in the late sixteenth century, church records are a remarkable source. Baptismal and burial records form the basis for family reconstitution, the basic process by which historical demographers reconstruct population history. Marriage registers provide historians with additional population data and with a record of who could, and could not, sign the register at marriage. The maps on pages 117 and 118, which show male and female literacy rates in France for the periods 1686-1690 and 1786-1790, are based on just such data. You may choose to reproduce these maps for use in a discussion of literacy rates or historical methodology.

The significance of the signature is, in fact, a current matter of debate among historians that may also be of interest to students. Does the act of signing constitute evidence of an individual's ability to read, and thus of his or her capacity to receive new ideas by way of the printed word? Historians have always assumed so, and the literacy evidence in this chapter is founded on that assumption. But a work by the French scholar Jean Quéniart (*Culture et société urbaines dans la France de l'Ouest au XVIIIe siècle,* 1978) has analyzed not just the quantity of signatures but their quality. Quéniart found many signatures so ill formed as to suggest no literacy in the signers. He also found documents signed with an "X" and the notation that the signer could not sign because he did not have with him his model signature from which to copy, a discovery suggesting that other signers also could not read and simply copied a signature from a card. Quéniart concluded that records of signatures probably somewhat overstate literacy rates. This conclusion drew immediate challenge from various quarters. Some historians, noting that elementary reading ability is easier to teach than penmanship, which requires close instructional supervision, have suggested that rates of signatures may actually understate literacy rates. Another group of historians, citing nineteenth-century French army draft records that demonstrate both literacy and the ability to sign, contend that the traditional correlation between signing and reading is a valid one.

The judges left us court records in which many of the persons involved in a proceeding were expected to sign, another indicator of the level of education that students can analyze in this chapter. Many courts adjudicated property disputes and registered deeds and wills, and such tribunals provide us with evidence of individual levels of wealth in a society. And in Continental European countries, legal officials known as notaries recorded wills, property transfers, and marriage settlements, providing an additional rich source of individual levels of wealth. One use of court records that is not illustrated

Percentage of spouses who signed their marriage licenses (1686–1690)

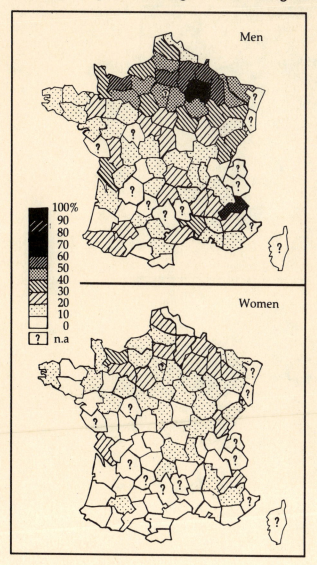

Percentage of spouses who signed their marriage licenses (1786–1790)

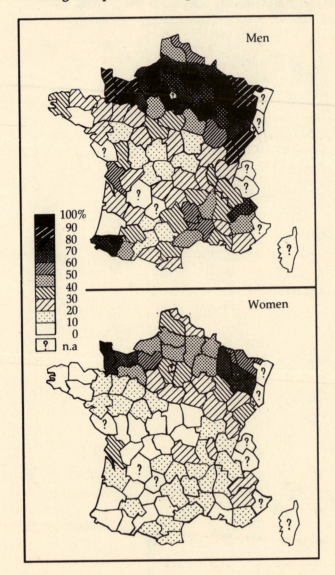

in this chapter's evidence involves reconstructing the social history of a group through criminal court records of local crime and conflict.

Police authorities in early modern Europe further added to our knowledge of the lives of the illiterate majority. Most Western governments recognized the correlation among food shortages, the resulting elevated market prices, and civil disorder. As a result, the law enforcement branches of many governments regulated market conditions and kept elaborate records of prices for such necessities as flour. From these records historians have been able to reconstruct the fluctuation of food prices in the seventeenth and eighteenth centuries. When food price data are combined with wage records, also often available in police records, historians can vividly describe the lifestyle of the poor.

The Evidence

Each piece of evidence in this chapter has been selected to assist students in answering the chapter's central questions. Each source may also provide a springboard for extended discussion that can strengthen students' understanding of early modern society.

Sources 1, 2, 3, and 4 concern agriculture and diet. You may wish to discuss modern diet in the West and to note such diverse effects of dietary deficiencies as delay of sexual maturity, reduced height, and incidence of nutritionally based ailments like rickets. The chapter's questions will guide students to the main conclusions suggested by these figures, but you can extend the discussion of these sources by posing additional questions. What effect might lower agricultural productivity have had on the long-term economic development of eastern Europe? Are some modern regions of the globe still governed by agricultural cycles similar to those that affected seventeenth- and eighteenth-century Europe?

Sources 5 through 10 present students with evidence of the level of public health in early modern Europe. Students should especially be guided to understanding the precarious nature of life, demonstrated by the frequency of demographic crises, the cost of epidemics, and the cycle of mortalities within the year. We have found that a highly effective way to stimulate students to think about this pre-industrial age lifestyle is to contrast early modern life expectancies with those of the modern world:

	Male	*Female*
United States (1989)	71.8 years	78.5 years
France (1989)	72.0	80.0
Guinea (1989)	40.0	4.0
Chad (1989)	38.0	40.0

Students will find average life expectancies in early modern Europe at or below the norms for the poorest Third World countries today.

Sources 11 and 12 should reinforce students' finding that the cycles of the agricultural year ruled many aspects of life for the early modern European majority. Here again you may wish to extend discussion to conditions in the modern Third World.

Questions to Consider

Source-specific questions in the Sources and Method section and general questions in Questions to Consider should direct students to a better understanding of rural life. To this end, you certainly will wish to summarize the chapter's evidence, but you may also want to reinforce students' analytical skills by asking them about the limitations of the sources we have used. What is it that we cannot know about early modern Europeans? What are the limits of collective biography?

Epilogue and Evaluation

The epilogue describes how the rural world presented in the chapter came to disappear in the West. We identify the roles of the Agricultural and Industrial Revolutions in this process, but you may wish to use the epilogue as a starting point for a general discussion of the nineteenth-century modernization process. A fundamental work you may wish to consult for background is Eugen Weber's *Peasants into Frenchmen: The Modernization of Rural France, 1870–1914* (1976). Weber identifies the full range of developments breaking down rural peasant isolation, including such factors as universal public education, improved transportation, and universal military service.

Evaluation may take many forms in this chapter. In classroom discussion, you may pose questions that require students to draw on the statistical material for their answers. For example, you may point out to them that the sixteenth and seventeenth centuries witnessed a number of witch hunts. What in the cultural and material levels of the people of these countries helps to account for such outbreaks of mass hysteria? In essay questions, you may ask students to describe the lifestyle and outlook of the early modern peasant farmer in any number of ways.

For Further Reading

R. J. Bernard, "Peasant Diet in Eighteenth-Century Gévaudan," in *European Diet from Preindustrial to Modern Times,* ed. Elborg and Robert Forster (1975). A good regional French example of pre-industrial era diet.

Marc Bloch, *French Rural History: An Essay on Its Basic Characteristics,* trans. Janet Sondheimer (1966). First published in 1929, this work by one of France's most distinguished historians represents the first modern scholarly effort at total historical understanding of the world of rural Europe.

Michael W. Flinn, *The European Demographic System, 1500–1820* (1981). Probably the best brief summary in English of recent scholarship.

François Furet and Jacques Ozouf, *Reading and Writing: Literacy in France from Calvin to Jules Ferry* (1982). The basic study of French literacy.

Pierre Goubert, *The French Peasantry in the Seventeenth Century* (1986). A general study by a master of population history.

Harvey J. Graff (ed.), *Literacy and Social Development in the West: A Reader* (1981). A collection of literacy studies covering Europe and America.

Peter Laslett, *The World We Have Lost Further Explored: England Before the Industrial Age* (1984). The latest edition of the pioneering work in English historical demography.

Emmanuel Le Roy Ladurie, *Times of Feast, Times of Famine: A History of Climate Since the Year 1000* (1971). A talented French historian's work on climatic history.

Michael Mitterauer and Reinhard Seider, *The European Family: Patriarchy and Partnership from the Middle Ages to the Present* (1982). Family history from the German and central European perspective.

B. H. Slicker van Bath, *The Agrarian History of Western Europe,* A.D. *500–1850* (1963). A fundamental study of Western agriculture, by a Dutch expert.

J. Dennis Willigan and Katherine A. Lynch, *Sources and Methods of Historical Demography* (1982). A comprehensive methodological work in English.

E. A. Wrigley and R. S. Schofield, *The Population History of England, 1541–1871* (1981). The product of numerous local population studies, this is a key work in English population history.

CHAPTER FIVE

A Day in the French Revolution: July 14, 1789

The French Revolution can sometimes be a difficult topic for both instructors and students. On one hand, instructors view the Revolution at a level of detail usually too extensive to include in a survey course in which only a few lectures can be devoted to events in France from 1789 to 1799. On the other hand, students often confront a textbook that describes the Revolution in terms too broad to convey more than a superficial impression of the issues and circumstances that caused it.

Chapter 5 provides an opportunity to guide students to a deeper understanding of the Revolution through a case study of Paris at the time of the attack on the Bastille. The chapter presents a variety of evidence that permits students to enter into the atmosphere in Paris leading up to this momentous event. By performing this exercise in historical reconstruction, they should be able to gain a more sophisticated perspective on the factors leading to the outbreak of the French Revolution.

The Problem

Content objectives:

1. to understand the general financial and political crisis confronting the monarchy of Louis XVI from 1787 to 1789

2. to understand the reasons for the Third Estate's defiance of the king and its reconstitution as the National Assembly

3. to learn how the general crisis of 1787 to 1789 and the Third Estate's actions affected the population of Paris

4. to understand the specific fears of Parisians during the month of July 1789

5. to identify those features of the eighteenth-century urban environment that enabled the rapid spread of popular unrest through certain districts of Paris, precipitating the assault on the Bastille

6. to extend the example of the Bastille assault to other great days of popular unrest during the Revolution as a foundation for understanding the popular dimensions of this national revolt

Skills objectives:

1. to analyze physical evidence to understand how environment may help to shape events

2. to analyze simple statistical data, expressed in tables, graphs, and maps, and to draw conclusions from these data relevant to events of 1789

3. to understand the variety of sources available to historians in reconstructing an event such as the assault on the Bastille, and the value and limitations of those sources

Beyond the topic of the French Revolution, this chapter may serve as the basis for discussion of broad issues such as the following:

1. How do crowd actions arise?

2. How do the reasons behind the crowd's attack on the Bastille differ from those of modern crowd actions?

3. Have there been other instances in history in which mass actions by crowds have greatly affected the course of events?

Sources and Method

This chapter presents students with a detailed episode of the French Revolution, and they may well wonder why. You can answer that question, while highlighting the importance of this chapter, in several ways.

You could begin by reviewing the historical study of crowd actions. Generations of middle-class historians shared the view of eighteenth- and nineteenth-century law enforcers that the crowd—or "mob," as they often negatively described it—was made up of society's lowest orders, those with nothing to lose who naturally inclined to crime and blind mayhem. This was the group that early modern French authorities often dismissed as *la lie du peuple* ("the scum of the people"). Only in the second half of this century, in work pioneered by George Rudé, have historians begun to understand the composition and motivations of the early modern crowd. Using police archives and other records, they have determined that the poorest elements in society seldom constituted the crowd. Rather, those persons with something to lose—individuals belonging to the middling orders of society—most often lent their numbers to crowd actions. Historians have also found that crowds rarely acted blindly. Instead, certain ideological considerations, usually defensive rather than revolutionary in inspiration, often provided the stimulus for crowd actions.

This framework should guide students in interpreting the chapter's data and, more essentially, should show them the importance of searching out the motivations of crowd members. When these underlying reasons are revealed, students will gain an informed understanding of the causes of the Revolution of 1789.

You may next wish to underscore the importance of crowd actions in modern history. The taking of the Bastille destroyed the resolution King Louis XVI initially made to resist calls for change. Crowd actions in the Great Fear of August 1789 prompted the National Assembly to restructure French society along more egalitarian lines. Crowd actions during the October Days of 1789 brought the king and the National Assembly to Paris from Versailles and thus placed them under the domination of the Paris masses. Further crowd actions toppled the monarchy in August 1792 and led to the bloody September Massacres later that year. The Revolution of 1789 was shaped by the crowds, and crowd actions were also to prove crucial in the European revolutions of 1830 and 1848.

The Evidence

Students again are confronted with various types of evidence in answering this chapter's central questions. You may wish to help them by discussing the sources in class.

Sources 1 through 4 are pictorial records of eighteenth-century Paris. You should remind students that this was an age without modern transportation and that most people walked to work. As a result, Paris, like most other European cities, was densely populated within the confines of its medieval walls. Students should be encouraged to place the evidence within this larger reality. Only then, for example, can they understand the attraction that the open green space of the Palais Royal held for Parisians and the speed with which rumors spread in densely populated neighborhoods.

Sources 5 and 6 are essential to answering the chapter's main questions but also to understanding the crisis of 1787 to 1789. Encourage students to remember that the elevated food prices affected not just Paris but all of France.

Source 7 reminds students of the lifestyle of the illiterate majority whose world they explored in Chapter 4. Bread was, indeed, the staff of life. Here students should be guided to note both the effect of price increases on a worker's budget and the social groups that were hardest hit by these increases.

Source 8 gives students their first exposure to a map as a means of transmitting statistical data. You may wish to orient students by pointing out some of the Parisian landmarks of the revolutionary period: Notre Dame Cathedral is on the Île de la Cité (the largest of the three islands in the Seine); the Louvre and Tuileries palace complex are at number 1 on the map; the Hôtel des Invalides is to the right of number 38; and the Champ-de-Mars (site of the Festival of the Federation in 1790 and of a massacre by Lafayette's National Guard in 1791) is the open space to the left of number 38. The main function of the map, however, is to develop student skills in interpreting data; this map will provide students with crucial social and economic data on the Bastille's assailants. Map reading is an important skill that is also used in other exercises in this volume.

Sources 9 and 10 should help students focus on faces in the crowd. You may wish to amplify the picture of the Bastille's attackers in Source 9 by reminding students that journeymen or apprentices (shown in parentheses) were not nearly as well compensated as most self-employed masters. You may also recall for students the range of incomes represented by the trades in Source 7. The essential message here, however, is that most of the attackers had some stake in society.

Source 10 shows students that women participated in the Revolution. You may wish to emphasize their role by describing for students the events of October 1789. Those "October Days" began with unrest among women confronting high food prices in the markets and culminated in the successful demands by Parisian crowds that forced the king and National Assembly to take up residence in Paris, not Versailles. The role of women is examined not only in the work by Darline Gay Levy and her colleagues from which Source 10 is taken but also in a study by Olwen Hufton (see For Further Reading).

Sources 11, 12, and 13 should lend detail to students' understanding of Parisian events. They also provide an opportunity for you as instructor to discuss the utility and limitations of diaries and correspondence as historical sources.

Questions to Consider

The questions posed in the chapter should lead students to a fuller understanding of the French Revolution. You may wish to pose broader questions in your discussion. Could some of the conditions leading to the events of July 1789 recur? Ask the students to draw especially on the knowledge of eighteenth-century agriculture they gained in Chapter 4 in examining the problem of food shortages. What about the fear motivating Parisians in July 1789? Did such anxieties not impel Frenchmen to take up arms in the Great Fear of 1789, the October Days, and the September Massacres? Your questions should take the most profitable direction of leading students to generalize from the Parisian experience of 1789. The result, in our experience, adds even more depth of perspective to students' understanding of the dynamics of the Revolution.

Epilogue and Evaluation

The purpose of the epilogue is to allow students to view the fall of the Bastille in the light of subsequent historical events. You may wish to use the epilogue as your starting point for a discussion of the significance of the chain of events initiated by the Bastille's fall. You may wish especially to treat the social revolution set in motion by the taking of the Bastille, and you could profitably contrast the society of Old Regime France with that of France after July 1789. You can make this comparison simply by concentrating on the events occurring in the immediate wake of the Bastille's fall: the "Glorious Night of August 4," during which the National Assembly abolished noble and clerical privilege; and the adoption of the Declaration of the Rights of Man and Citizen on August 26, 1789. The Declaration of the Rights of Man and Citizen can be a particularly useful instrument in enhancing students' understanding of the changes wrought by the Revolution. It is readily available in English (in, for example, the appendix to Georges Lefebvre's *The Coming of the French Revolution*) and can be either read or distributed to the class as a basis for additional discussion.

Several opportunities are open to the instructor in evaluating student comprehension of this chapter. The central questions may be used as a written assignment or as an examination or quiz question. An especially effective evaluation tool is a question for class discussion or an essay that asks: "Imagine yourself a master cabinetmaker of the Faubourg Saint-Antoine. What was your lifestyle like in July 1789? What did you know about political and economic developments at that time? How did you respond?"

For Further Reading

Richard Mowery Andrews, "Paris of the Great Revolution, 1789–1796," in *People and Communities in the Western World,* ed. Gene Brucker (1979). An excellent brief sketch of late-eighteenth-century Paris and its revolutionary role.

David Garrioch, *Neighbourhood and Community in Paris, 1740–1790* (1986). An important recent study of Parisian society in the late eighteenth century.

Jacques Godechot, *The Taking of the Bastille, July 14, 1789,* trans. Jean Stewart (1970). A study of the Bastille's fall by one of France's greatest twentieth-century students of the Revolution.

Olwen Hufton, "Women in Revolution," *Past and Present* 53 (1971): 90–108. Examines the participation of women in the French Revolution.

Steven L. Kaplan, *The Famine Plot Persuasion in Eighteenth-Century France* (1982). A work important in understanding the connection between dearth and crowd actions.

Jeffry Kaplow, *The Names of Kings: The Parisian Laboring Poor in the Eighteenth Century* (1972). A study of the world of the Parisian poor: their living condition, attitudes, and beliefs.

Georges Lefebvre, *The Coming of the French Revolution,* trans. R. R. Palmer (1947). A brief study of the opening days of the French Revolution through October 1789 by a master of the history of the Revolution.

Darline Gay Levy, Harriet Branson Applewhite, and Mary Durham Johnson (eds. and trans.), *Women in Revolutionary Paris 1789–1795* (1979). A collection of primary sources revealing the role of women in the Revolution.

Daniel Roche, *The People of Paris: An Essay in Popular Culture in the Eighteenth Century,* trans. Marie Evans (1987). An admirable re-creation of the life of Parisian common people.

Daniel Roche (ed.), *Journal of My Life* by Jacques-Louis Ménétra (1986). The earthy autobiography of a Parisian glassworker of the revolutionary period.

George Rudé, *The Crowd in the French Revolution* (1959). This work is the foundation of historians' modern understanding of the composition of crowds.

E. P. Thompson, "The Moral Economy of the English Crowd in the Eighteenth Century," *Past and Present* 50 (1971): 76–136. Another pioneering work in understanding early modern crowd actions, in this case food riots.

Michelle Vovelle, *The Fall of the French Monarchy, 1787–1792*, trans. Susan Burke (1984). A recent general study of the Revolution's early years.

CHAPTER SIX

Labor Old and New: The Impact of the Industrial Revolution

One of our students once wrote, with fractured historical logic, "The nineteenth century was a long century." From the instructor's viewpoint, this remark could not have been more correct. That century produced the Industrial Revolution, much of the ideological orientation of the modern West, the imperialism that by 1914 brought half of the earth's land area under European governance, and a great deal more. Inevitably, instructors and the textbooks they use devote piecemeal attention to all of these developments but extensive treatment to none.

In the case of the Industrial Revolution, nearly all textbooks now include testimony or pictorial excerpts from the reports of the Sadler Committee or other bodies investigating working conditions. Nevertheless, accounts of technological developments or statistical data on rising mine and mill output often obscure the great human cost of industrial change. As instructors in traditional Western Civilization courses, we too have struggled with the problem of giving adequate coverage to every aspect of industrialization in academic sessions of fixed durations. The present chapter is our attempt at a comprehensive yet compact body of readings emphasizing the human toll of industrialization. The contrast in working conditions between the preindustrial and industrial eras offers students stark evidence of the human dimension of industrialization.

The Problem

Content objectives:

1. to understand the nature of preindustrial production

2. to learn about working conditions in the traditional European economy

130

3. to comprehend the changes in work organization that constituted the process economic historians call proto-industrialization

4. to understand the nature of industrial production

5. to learn about the working conditions of industrial production

6. to examine the impact of the transformation in working conditions on industrial-age workers

Skills objectives:

1. to analyze such nontraditional historical evidence as popular songs and lists of holidays in order to derive relevant historical data from these sources

2. to analyze materials such as guild regulations, factory work rules, and contracts for their historical message

3. to gain familiarity with the legislative hearings reports generated by modern governments in order to draw a historical message from this important type of source

Sources and Method

We have grouped the evidence in this chapter in a fashion that permits students to compare the nature of labor in the preindustrial and industrial eras, and the chapter's central questions guide students in that comparison. Our approach takes its lead from the recent work by those social and economic historians of the Industrial Revolution whose works are listed at the end of the chapter.

We have found the comparative approach to be highly stimulating for late-twentieth-century students, who have seldom reflected on the relatively recent advent of the modern industrial age with its time clock, production line, and more recent computer-generated analyses of productivity. One of us, who also teaches an interdisciplinary course in history and philosophy, has had particular success in eliciting student response on the issue of industrial discipline by introducing the thought of the late philosopher Michel Foucault. We present Foucault's view that the asylum, the penitentiary, and the factory are all simply different features of the same drive to create the modern disciplined society. Although we share with many of our historian colleagues reservations about Foucault's historical methods, we have used his ideas as a most effective instrument in generating student thought and discussion. You may find the general outlines of Foucault's thought in one of his best-known works, *Discipline and Punish: The Birth of the Prison* (1977).

A broad discussion of the industrial age originating in Foucault can merge easily into discussion of the chapter's central questions. The first question asks students to compare preindustrial and industrial labor. We have found it worthwhile to aid students in this task by a brief general discussion of Old Regime society, highlighting its corporate nature and especially the importance of guilds. You may also wish to recall for students the difficulties of agricultural life portrayed in Chapter 4.

The second main question asks how industrial labor evolved. You may wish to emphasize for students that early modern developments in work organization helped to pave the way for the Industrial Revolution. Most economic historians view this process of "proto-industrialization" as an essential step toward industrialization. When it is put in such a context, students should be able to appreciate readily the implications of the "putting-out" system of textile production described by La Rochefoucauld-Liancourt (Source 5) for traditional production modes described in guild regulations (Source 4).

The final question asks students to consider the impact of modern industrial labor on workers. Students should be encouraged to look for effects not only in wages, hours, and working conditions but also in the psychological toll paid by the first generation of workers who encountered the discipline of the modern workplace.

The Evidence

As with earlier chapters in this book, students will benefit from a brief discussion of the sources. This discussion not only should emphasize the specific task at hand—that is, answering the chapter's central questions from the sources—but also should develop in students a feel for the uses of the primary materials that historians work with in their studies.

We have divided this chapter's sources into two groups: the first (Sources 1 through 6) deals with preindustrial labor; the second (Sources 7 through 11) treats labor in the Industrial Revolution. Sources 1 and 2 focus on agricultural labor. Encourage your students to examine these sources critically to determine conditions of work, pay, and worker satisfaction with the employment. Note particularly that Mrs. Britton in Source 2 has a basis for comparing industrial and agricultural work.

Sources 3 and 4 deal with the work of urban, preindustrial craftspeople. Source 3 offers students a calendar of work holidays in seventeenth-century

Lille. Many of the religious observances on this list will mean little to students, even to many of those who are Roman Catholic in faith. The risk here is that students will give the calendar only a cursory glance and move on quickly to the other reading. Encourage the students instead to consider the calendar thoughtfully. How many days per year might a Lille textile worker be expected to labor? How frequently was the schedule of Lille workers interrupted by a respite from labor? Remind students that much of early modern Europe worked on such a schedule.

You should encourage this same questioning attitude as students approach Source 4. Here they should not just accomplish the easy task—noting the details of guild labor—but should proceed to the more challenging task of determining the kind of economic relationships that guild regulations sought to maintain.

Sources 5 and 6 present perspectives on the process of proto-industrialization. Students should determine here what kinds of production and business methods were emerging in the later years of preindustrial textile production. How would these methods facilitate industrialization?

In Sources 7 and 8 the student will read actual work rules for early industrial workers. Encourage students to contrast this style of work with preindustrial labor. Most important, ask them to analyze from these documents the type of discipline management sought to elicit and the ways in which that discipline was enforced. Students should use the same mode of analysis in Source 10, the record of an observer of German female textile workers. What kind of discipline applied in these mills? What kind of work conditions?

Sources 2, 9, and 11 offer the students their first encounter with a type of record that Western democracies produced in great volume during the nineteenth and twentieth centuries, the records of hearings by legislative bodies. You may wish to emphasize the great utility of such sources for the historian. Secretaries often recorded verbatim the testimony given to legislative committees, and the result is another record of the thoughts and activities of the illiterate majority of the early modern world that left little written record of its experiences. What kind of conditions did workers endure?

Questions to Consider

This section poses highly focused questions to guide students' understanding of the chapter's evidence. You may wish to build on these foundations by asking students to generalize on what they have learned. Was the Industrial Revolution strictly a nineteenth-century phenomenon? Aren't Third World societies experiencing similarly wrenching social changes as a result of their rapid twentieth-century industrialization? What sort of structural economic changes are bringing disturbing changes to the workplace of the twentieth-century West?

Epilogue and Evaluation

In the epilogue we endeavor to take students beyond the early Industrial Revolution into modern times. We show how political developments and the right of labor to organize and strike contributed to improved wages and working conditions, but we also stress that the basic working conditions of industrial workers remain in essence unchanged. They still lack the relative autonomy of their preindustrial ancestors despite widely publicized efforts to move industrial production beyond the production line. You may wish to expand this point to emphasize the importance of the Industrial Revolution in defining the West's work life. In such a discussion, you might draw, as we do, on the 1968 industrial unrest in France that called attention to enduring and deep-seated worker discontent with modern industrial employment. Such an approach has the added benefit of preparing students for a fuller examination of the events of 1968 in Chapter 14. You could also discuss current experiments in moving the manufacturing of certain products beyond the rigid production-line style of assembly.

Evaluation can be accomplished in several ways. We prefer a debate format for small class sections: Ask the students to take sides in a debate on the positive and negative consequences of industrialization. You may even wish to amplify students' activities by assigning them selections on the historical debate about whether industrialization improved or worsened the Western standard of living in the nineteenth century (see For Further Reading for suggestions). For larger class sections, an essay question may easily be constructed around the central theme of this chapter: the contrast between preindustrial and industrial labor.

For Further Reading

Ronald M. Hartwell, *The Industrial Revolution and Economic Growth* (1971). A collection of essays by the author, including several that highlight historians' debates on whether industrialization improved or worsened the standard of living in early-nineteenth-century England.

E. J. Hobsbawm, *Labouring Men* (1964). Essays by the author on early industrial work and the standard-of-living debate.

David S. Landes, *The Unbound Prometheus: Technological Change and Industrial Development in Western Europe from 1750 to the Present* (1970). The foremost history of the technological changes that transformed the early-nineteenth-century West.

Ivy Pinchbeck, *Women Workers and the Industrial Revolution,* 1750–1850 (1930). An old but classic examination of women's work in England.

Sidney Pollard, "Factory Discipline in the Industrial Revolution," *Economic History Review,* 16 (1963): 254–271. An excellent article on the disciplining of early industrial workers.

James S. Roberts, *Drink, Temperance and the Working Class in Nineteenth-Century Germany* (1984). A treatment of the alcohol problem in the context of the Industrial Revolution.

George Rudé, *The Crowd in History,* 1730–1848 (1964). This important study of crowd violence focuses in part on the Luddite phenomenon.

Joan W. Scott, *The Glassworkers of Carmaux: French Craftsmen and Political Action in a Nineteenth-Century City* (1974). A study of French glassworkers as the Industrial Revolution transformed their work from a skilled craft to an occupation within an increasingly mechanized industry.

Joan W. Scott and Louise A. Tilly, *Women, Work, and Family* (1978). An excellent study of the evolution of female work in England and France.

William H. Sewell, Jr., *Work and Revolution in France: The Language of Labor from the Old Regime to 1848* (1980). An important reconstruction of the world of French artisans in the early years of the modern capitalist system.

K. D. M. Snell, *Annals of the Labouring Poor: Social Change and Agrarian England, 1669–1900* (1985). An excellent treatment of rural southern England that traces the declining circumstances of the region's workers in the age of industrialization.

E. P. Thompson, *The Making of the English Working Class* (1963). A massive study of the formation of the English working class.

E. P. Thompson, "Time, Work Discipline and Industrial Capitalism," *Past and Present* 38 (1967): 56–97. A pioneering article on the new concepts of time discipline that were introduced by industrialization.

Nancy Tomes, "A Torrent of Abuse: Crimes of Violence Between Working-Class Men and Women in London, 1840–1875," *Journal of Social History* 11 (1977–1978): 328–345. An examination of working-class domestic violence that reveals widespread peer group toleration of the problem.

CHAPTER SEVEN

Two Programs for Social and Political Change: Liberalism and Socialism

It was once common for historians to introduce their students to the nineteenth century by noting that it was the century of "isms." The instructor would then duly note the rise of romanticism, industrialism, liberalism, socialism, and imperialism during the century, all justifying his or her assertion. This characterization of the century is indeed incontrovertible, and the second volume of *Discovering the Western Past* does explore a number of "isms," including industrialism (Chapter 6), imperialism (Chapter 9), and the present chapter's subjects, liberalism and socialism.

Chapter 7 is the second chapter in Volume II to explore political ideology. Devoting two chapters to political thought reflects our view that such "traditional" history is essential to students' understanding of certain periods of the past. Just as the treatment of the theoretical and physical expressions of absolutism in Chapter 2 provided the framework for examining the government and society of the early modern period, we believe that close study of the topics in Chapter 7 is essential to a comprehensive understanding of the industrial age.

In Chapter 7 students examine the proposals for political, economic, and social change put forward first by nineteenth-century liberals, exemplified by Alexis de Tocqueville, and then by Karl Marx and his socialist adherents. We believe that this chapter will fill a gap in many textbooks' treatments of the nineteenth century. Almost all give considerable attention to Marx and his economic thought; other aspects of Marx's thought and the whole subject of nineteenth-century liberalism are often passed over, however. Chapter 7 offers fuller coverage of liberalism and socialism than is provided in most textbooks. We present the ideological clashes of the nineteenth century by means of detailed background on liberalism, socialism, Tocqueville, and Marx in The Problem and Sources and Method sections of the chapter. These introductions are followed by selections from Tocqueville and Marx that address the same basic issues, permitting students to compare the two men's ideas.

137

The Problem

Content objectives:

1. to understand the basic ideological positions of nineteenth-century liberals as exemplified by Alexis de Tocqueville

2. to understand the basic ideological positions of Karl Marx and the movement he inspired

3. to trace the influence of these ideologies on the history of nineteenth-century politics

Skills objectives:

1. to analyze written materials on political and social theories

2. to make a comparative analysis of such theories as a means of understanding the main ideological currents of an age

Sources and Method

We have arranged evidence in this chapter by author, but the selections from the authors' works present their respective views on the same topics: the nature of historical change, revolution in general and the specific Revolution of 1848 in France, and the ideal form of government. An additional selection from Tocqueville also examines problems inherent in democracy.

Students are, as usual, directed in their analysis of the evidence by basic questions posed at the end of The Problem section: What visions of the future did liberals and socialists propose? How did they hope to realize their ideals? How did their ideologies differ? These general questions are supplemented by sharply focused questions in the Sources and Method section. You may wish to offer your students guidance in formulating answers by asking them to recall the sweeping social and economic changes wrought by industrialization, and you may wish to preview here the societal problems created by the urbanization whose final stages are the subject of Chapter 8.

Keeping in mind the deep gulf between rich and poor, students should be able to gain some insight into the main ideological currents of the nineteenth century. Liberalism represented the ideas of the majority of the governing and managerial groups; socialism was the ideology of increasing numbers of industrial workers.

The Evidence

As we noted, the chapter presents the thinking of Tocqueville and Marx on the same basic issues, and it may thus be presented to students in the form of a debate. Successful use of this chapter, we believe, requires that students be able to grasp the basic ideas of these two figures, and nothing is more crucial to that task than comprehending their individual visions of historical change.

You might introduce the whole problem of historical change in discussing basic theories of history with students. Do historians discern patterns in history? Is history a science? Your choice of authorities to cite in such a discussion is immense, but you might profitably introduce the pattern of change (thesis-antithesis-synthesis) propounded by Georg Hegel as a starting point that also will serve to clarify the origins of Marxist historical thought. You may also wish to discuss those historians who attempt to identify cycles in history, including Oswald Spengler (*The Decline of the West,* 2 vols., 1918–1922), Arnold Toynbee (*A Study of History,* 12 vols., 1934–1961), and the more recent and fascinating work of Paul M. Kennedy (*The Rise and Fall of the Great Powers: Economic Change and Military Conflict from 1500 to 2000,* 1987). From such a general discussion you could then ask students to fit the patterns of historical development posited by de Tocqueville and Marx (in Sources 1 and 5) into the broader problem of historical change. Students should be able to identify readily the evolutionary vision of historical change set forth by Tocqueville and the rigid pattern of change described by the "scientific socialist," Marx.

Tocqueville saw an evolutionary trend toward greater democracy. But he was not an uncritical observer of the development, as Source 2, from his *Democracy in America,* demonstrates. We have found that students show a keen interest in Tocqueville's critique of American democracy. You have an excellent opportunity with this selection to expand the scope of classroom discussion by simply asking students whether Tocqueville's criticisms were valid in the nineteenth century and whether the problems he identified persist in American democracy today.

Tocqueville and Marx both wrote about the French Revolution of 1848, and Sources 3 and 6 present their respective views. You may wish to discuss the causes and course of that revolution so that students can place the ideas of Tocqueville and Marx in context. You will certainly wish to emphasize the basic attitudes of Tocqueville and Marx toward this revolution. Why did Tocqueville view the revolution as a tragedy? Why did Marx, despite the revolution's failure, regard it as a positive step?

Finally, Sources 4 and 7 offer students both authors' visions of their ideal governments. With these selections students' comprehension can be measured in how well they understand the two authors' theories as a natural extension of their thinking on the political realities of their age. You should reinforce the point that the positions of Tocqueville and Marx for the most part were representative of nineteenth-century liberal and socialist thought, respectively. You may emphasize the potentials for change in both of these visions by contrasting them in class discussion with the historical situation in Europe at the midpoint of the nineteenth century.

Questions to Consider

This section poses the usual questions directly related to the sources. The questions also offer you a good foundation from which to move beyond the mid-nineteenth-century setting of this chapter. To accomplish this, you may ask additional questions that lead students to think about the nineteenth century as a whole. How did English liberals find an evolutionary path toward greater political democracy? Why were liberals in England, Italy, Germany, and other countries able to accept monarchy as their system of government? These and other broader considerations may prompt students to recognize the impact of the ideologies represented by Tocqueville and Marx on the history of the nineteenth century.

Epilogue and Evaluation

All of our epilogues are designed to take the student beyond the chapter's material and thereby enhance his or her understanding of the larger issues posed by the sources. This epilogue is no exception, but in the interests of a stimulating classroom discussion you might build on the material that the text presents.

We like to emphasize that much of twentieth-century ideology was born in the nineteenth century. Students can trace the ideas of liberals into the twentieth century and decide, for example, whether these ideas have a kinship to twentieth-century U.S. conservatism. Similarly, they can follow the implementation of Marx's ideas to determine why they did not work out as Marx predicted. Perhaps students can discuss the modifications of Marxist thought currently under way in the People's Republic of China and the failure of Marxism in the former Soviet Union.

The material in this chapter is conveniently arranged for a debate. Consider dividing the class into "liberal" and "socialist" groups in order to assess students' comprehension of the chapter's material by the answers they offer to specific nineteenth-century problems you present. Topics might include the desirability of mass political participation and the regulation of industrial wages and hours, as well as other issues of the age. For larger class sections, essay examinations may be built around liberal and Marxist thought or the Revolution of 1848.

For Further Reading

Maurice Agulhon, *The Republican Experiment, 1848–1852,* trans. Janet Lloyd (1983). A modern study of the era of the Revolution of 1848 in France.

Julius Braunthal, *History of the International* (1980). A good study of Marxist attempts at organization.

C. A. Cohen, *Karl Marx's Theory of History: A Defense* (1978). A philosopher's careful examination of one of the central aspects of Marx's thought.

Georges Duveau, 1848: *The Making of a Revolution,* trans. Anne Carter (1966). An excellent detailed study of the events of February through June 1848 in Paris.

Edward T. Gargan, *Alexis de Tocqueville: The Critical Years, 1848–1851* (1951). A study of Tocqueville during the period of the Revolution of 1848 and the Napoleonic seizure of power.

Oscar J. Hammen, *The Red '48-ers* (1968). Marx and Engels in the Revolution of 1848.

Warren Lerner, *A History of Socialism and Communism in Modern Times: Theorists, Activists, and Humanists* (1982). A very useful modern survey.

George Lichtheim, *Marxism: An Historical and Critical Study* (1982). A thoughtful analysis of Marxist doctrine.

Jack Lively, *The Social and Political Thought of Alexis de Tocqueville* (1962). An excellent examination of Tocqueville's thoughts on liberty, social and political democracy, centralization of government, religion, and revolution.

David McLellan, *Karl Marx: His Life and Thought* (1973). A detailed biography.

Guido de Ruggiero, *The Story of European Liberalism* (1927). Its comparative examination of English, French, German, and Italian liberalism makes this older study a valuable reference tool.

CHAPTER EIGHT

Vienna and Paris, 1850–1930: The Development of the Modern City

Between the years 1850 and 1930 the Western city as we know it took shape as European cities broke the restraints of their medieval walls to assume their modern physical form and to create the municipal services of present-day urban centers. The history of this urban development is a fascinating excursion in social history that often is missing from the standard curriculum. Most survey textbooks devote only a few cursory paragraphs to urban development, and only the larger educational institutions have the resources to offer coursework in urban history. We therefore endeavor in Chapter 8 to offer students a sample of the absorbing work of the historian of cities as we explore Western urban history in the period 1850 to 1930.

The Problem

Content objectives:

1. to understand the impact of industrialization and population growth on European cities in the early nineteenth century

2. to examine the opportunities for urban improvement created by the Industrial Revolution

3. to trace the development of the modern Western city in the industrial age

Skills objectives:

1. to analyze pictorial evidence for relevant historical insights

2. to analyze such standard sources of urban history as city maps for information about the lifestyle of the population

3. to become familiar with architectural drawings and to analyze the design of public and private buildings for its underlying social message

4. to assemble the results of cartographic and pictorial analyses into an overview of nineteenth- and early-twentieth-century urban development

Sources and Method

This chapter employs a comparative approach to urban history, assembling evidence on Paris and Vienna, two of the largest western European cities of the late nineteenth and early twentieth centuries. We hope that students will analyze the evidence from these cities with the goal of discerning general trends in urban development. With urbanization, as with industrialization, we have found that late-twentieth-century students have rarely thought about the genesis of their own lifestyles.

In our own classes, we begin treatment of the material in this chapter with a general discussion of modern urban life based on the city in which our educational institution is located. We ask students basic questions about that city: What type of residential patterns does it have? Where are commercial and industrial zones located? What type of transportation system brings these zones together? What kinds of urban recreational opportunities does the city offer? What infrastructure for protecting the public health exists in the water and sanitary systems? How did such practices, facilities, and institutions develop? We follow up students' answers to such questions with brief descriptions of the history of our urban area to fill in gaps in student knowledge. Two of us, for example, teach in Milwaukee. The Milwaukee metropolitan area was linked until about four decades ago by a comprehensive interurban rail system—about which most students have no knowledge—that is important in understanding local urban development. Other cities have similar historical characteristics that may need to be pointed out.

Our general discussion of an urban area familiar to students moves naturally into a discussion of factors influencing all modern urban development, and this conveniently leads in turn to the central questions of Chapter 8. The first of those questions asks how city planners reshaped nineteenth-century Paris and Vienna in response to the problems posed by rapid industrial-age growth. We have found it useful to assist students in answering this question by briefly reviewing the social consequences of industrialization and by specifically calling their attention to the statistical evidence of urban population growth presented in the chapter.

The second main question asks students to describe the transformation in urban life resulting from the physical reshaping of cities. Students' success in answering this question may be enhanced if you pose certain analytical criteria, among them ascertaining how housing resources, health levels, and recreational opportunities were improved.

The Evidence

Chapter 8 is the first chapter in Volume II in which evidence is presented entirely in the form of pictures and maps. We have made exclusive use of pictorial evidence because it presents such a vital source for historians. The risk with illustrations, however, is that students will give the evidence only quick and casual attention. Consequently, we have posed general and specific questions that require close analysis of the illustrations. You may wish to pose additional questions that will anchor students' attention in the sources.

You may also promote close student attention to the illustrated sources by analyzing one example from each type. Sources 1 through 3, 5, 8, 9, 13, 14, 16, 18 through 21, and 24 are pictures with various general views of Paris and Vienna. Source 1, for example, is a picture of Vienna in 1850. Analyzing it with students can suggest to them the kinds of critical thinking you wish them to employ. Ask students questions such as: What was the probable population density of Vienna? What impeded its outward growth? What might life have been like within the city's walls?

Sources 4, 6, and 7 are maps. These may require a bit more attention from the instructor for successful student analysis. The current weakness of secondary school curricula in the field of geography makes it difficult for some students to interpret maps. Thus you might take Source 6, a rather complex map, as an example for class analysis. Have students identify the changes under way in Paris by asking them to trace the city's physical expansion. Also ask them to identify the transportation systems facilitating this growth, improvements in water supply, and the expansion of recreational opportunities.

Sources 10 through 12 and 15, 17, 22, and 23 illustrate the residential forms created in nineteenth-century and early-twentieth-century cities. Without doubt, the most challenging piece of evidence in this group will be Source 12, the floor plan of a Paris apartment block. You may wish to explain the nature of such nineteenth-century buildings to students, noting the interior courtyard with its stables and coach houses, the exterior shops on the ground floor, and the pattern of movement of residents past the concierge's lodge into the building. We provide the plan with a detailed key, but you may also wish to show students specifically what window and door openings look like on the plan. You might then ask the students to think about the building: What social group probably lived here (note such features as service stairs and the fact that the attic housed servants)? What sort of light did the architect afford many rooms? Are the standards of privacy we are accustomed to always available in the apartments shown in this floor plan? In this regard, we like to reflect with students on the relatively recent development in Western architecture of the corridor, which provides for privacy because individual rooms do not open onto one another.

Questions to Consider

The very specific questions in this section, designed to guide students' analysis and response to the chapter's central questions, can provide the foundation for more general discussion. At this juncture we like to expand the discussion by asking students to reflect on the ways in which the Industrial Revolution, which created so many of the problems of early-nineteenth-century urban life, also provided the means for their solution. Point to the rail lines, which alleviated urban crowding by allowing urban expansion, and the new wealth, which financed museums and other cultural opportunities newly opened to all. How many of these developments could have been realized without industrialization?

Ask students what other innovations were being introduced in the nineteenth century. At the same time that Haussmann was building a healthier Paris with an improved water system, parks, and broad streets, what was Louis Pasteur doing? This section can, in short, become your vehicle for tying together and highlighting for students the many significant changes brought to Western life by nineteenth-century developments.

Epilogue And Evaluation

Our epilogue takes the student into the middle twentieth century in the histories of Paris and Vienna. In concluding the chapter, you may choose to go still further. You may ask students about the late-twentieth-century problems confronting urban centers, highlighting such difficulties as the air pollution produced by modern industries and a transportation system increasingly reliant on the internal combustion engine. Airborne corrosive chemicals are eroding many of Europe's greatest architectural monuments. In North America and in Europe, "acid rain" threatens the environment as a whole. How will the next generation deal with such problems? Ask students to speculate on the changes their proposed solutions might bring to the urban industrialized West.

Evaluation of student mastery of this chapter's material may take several forms. In the context of a class discussion, one colleague of ours presents students who have mastered the general trends in urban history with a map of a nineteenth-century city they have not specifically studied. He asks students first to analyze the geographic features of the city and its region, the transportation system, and the industrial activities of the town in the year 1850. Then the students are asked to draw on their general knowledge to project trends in expansion and land use patterns. The discussion culminates in the presentation of a modern map of the city so that students may check their prognostications.

More traditional evaluation may take the form of an essay topic; for example, you might ask students to discuss the various improvements in European urban life that occurred during the second half of the nineteenth century, including the relationships of these improvements to the Industrial Revolution.

For Further Reading

Louis Chevalier, *Laboring Classes and Dangerous Classes in Paris During the First Half of the Nineteenth Century,* trans. Frank Jellinek (1973). A challenging but vivid description of the social problems of rapidly growing Paris in the years before the improvements of Napoleon III and Baron Haussmann.

Mark Girouard, *Cities and People: A Social and Architectural History* (1985). A well-illustrated general study.

Helmut Gruber, *Red Vienna: Experiment in Working-Class Culture, 1919–1934* (1991). A comprehensive study of socialist government in Vienna after World War I and its attempt to improve workers' material and cultural lives.

Paul M. Hohenberg and Lynn Hollen Lees, *The Making of Urban Europe, 1000–1950* (1985). A useful survey of European urban history.

Andrew Lees, *Cities Perceived: Urban Society in European and American Thought, 1820–1940* (1985). Concentrating on the period 1880 to 1914, this study examines Western thought about the city and its problems during a period of urban growth.

John P. McKay, *Tramways and Trolleys: The Rise of Urban Mass Transport in Europe* (1976). An important study of the social impact of urban mass transport.

John Merriman (ed.), *French Cities in the Nineteenth Century: Class, Power, and Urbanization* (1982). A collection of studies on the growth of major French urban centers.

Donald J. Olsen, *The City as a Work of Art: London, Paris, Vienna* (1986). A well-illustrated study of urban development.

David H. Pinkney, *Napoleon III and the Rebuilding of Paris* (1958). The fundamental study of the projects of Napoleon III and Baron Haussmann for modernizing nineteenth-century Paris.

Carl E. Schorske, *Fin-de-siècle Vienna: Politics and Culture* (1981). A study of Viennese culture with a long and important chapter on development of the Ringstrasse.

Paul White, *The West European City: A Social Geography* (1984). An excellent general study of European urban development, treating such topics as housing, residential patterns, population, and land use.

Howard Zehr, *Crime and the Development of Modern Society: Patterns of Criminality in Nineteenth-Century Germany and France* (1976). A challenging study of the impact of urbanization on crime patterns.

CHAPTER NINE

Expansion and Public Opinion: Advocates of The "New Imperialism"

In 1899 American editorialist and anti-imperialist Finley Peter Dunne (who spoke through the voice of his fictitious Irish-American character, Mr. Dooley) openly mocked many of the arguments used to justify imperialism:

> An' now, ye mis'rable, childish-minded apes, we propose f'r to larn ye th' uses iv liberty . . . an' we'll larn ye our language, because 'tis aisier to larn ye ours than to larn oursilves yours. An' we'll give ye clothes, if ye pay f'r them; an', if ye don't, ye can go without. . . . We can't give ye anny votes, because we haven't more thin enough to go round now; but we'll threat ye th' way a father shud threat his childhen if we have to break ivry bone in ye'er bodies. So come to our ar-rms, says we.

Dunne's lampooning of the "white man's burden," together with the more serious criticisms of imperialism by J. A. Hobson, Henry Labouchère, Mark Twain, Lenin, and others, seem to strike a responsive chord with our students, many of whom wonder how the advocates of the "new imperialism" could possibly have carried the day. Indeed, from our perspective, neoimperialist arguments appear egregiously self-serving, blatantly racist, and incredibly hypocritical. How could the spokespersons for imperialism possibly have been heeded more than those whom we see as the defenders of reason, justice, and morality? To be sure, characterizations like Dunne's are gross exaggerations, but they are ones often embraced by our students, men and women still capable of outrage and even, at certain moments, idealism.

Thus it is crucial for students to understand and appreciate the economic, demographic, political, and intellectual currents that the advocates of imperialism could draw on in their arguments, currents that ultimately fed into a new era of colonialism. It is also important to explain that the individual nations of western Europe embraced imperialism for different reasons and in response to different perceived needs. Yet, whatever the motives, in the end the West engaged in a scramble for colonies, a fact that brought Western nations into conflict with one another.

Students can also be helped to recognize one of the great ironies of the period, the fact that the "logical" and "rational" arguments of imperialism's advocates ultimately brought the West into the most irrational of situations: the Great War and (according to Hannah Arendt) totalitarianism. To solve specific pressing problems, the imperialists in turn created others, problems that brought the West into the dual maelstroms of the twentieth century.

The Problem

Content objectives:

1. to understand the trends and forces that led to the "new imperialism" and the ways in which this phenomenon differed, if at all, from its older forms

2. to understand the principal arguments of the advocates of imperialism

3. to foresee the probable results of that imperialism, in the short and long term, for both the host populations and the West itself

Skills objectives:

1. to summarize the main arguments of each speaker or writer

2. to link these arguments to the principal trends and temper of the time (including racism and other widespread attitudes)

3. to identify hyperbole and hypocrisy and to separate the real arguments for imperialism from the postured ones

On a larger scale, you may want your students to discuss some of the following questions:

1. The British often referred to non-Westerners as "wogs" (an acronym for "worthy Oriental gentlemen"). Why did Westerners usually view non-Western peoples as inferiors? To what extent does that view still prevail today? What have been the results of the West's persistence in holding that view?

2. Imperialism has been seen as a major contributing factor to the coming of World War I. How can this hypothesis be proved (or disproved)?

3. If public opinion had *not* been a factor (that is, if the advocates and foes of imperialism had not been forced to state their respective positions before an enlarged electorate), would Western policymakers have been so eager to embrace imperial adventuring? Why or why not?

4. What have been the residual effects of Western imperialism? That is, how has the West gained or lost because of its imperialistic ventures? Think especially of the world after 1945.

5. Besides controlling regions politically, in what other ways has the West practiced imperialism? What do you see as the principal differences or similarities between the imperialism of the nineteenth century and later imperialistic ventures?

6. To what extent does the West now depend on resources found in non-Western areas? How has the West responded to that problem? What residual effects has that response had?

Most of these questions are designed to lead to one central question: To what extent are the attitudes of imperialism still with us? Were its advocates so persuasive that, even after the empires have fallen, the attitudes and ideology that created them remain healthy? Indeed, this last question may be the most important of all.

Sources and Method

This section offers a good list of questions that students can use as they read the evidence. Before they approach the evidence, however, you will need to provide background information on:

1. The speaker or writer and his background. Supplement the biographical material with your own knowledge.

2. Some of the problems facing each speaker's nation and how these problems might have been used by the advocates of imperialism to argue for their cause. In other words, what was it that made citizens of each nation particularly vulnerable to the call for imperialism?

The Evidence

Most of us are used to reading works or listening to speeches that oblige us to sift through a great deal of bombast, hyperbole, hypocrisy, and outright falsehood to determine what the writer or speaker is really saying. In this chapter, however, students will be struck by the blatant forthrightness of the late-nineteenth-century advocates of imperialism, who rarely disguised arguments appealing to greed and racism. There will not be much need for students to read between the lines; the advocates' ideas seem to have been fairly widespread, thus eliminating the need for concealment. For example, referring to non-Western people today as uncivilized or barbaric is, to say the very least, considered bad form. Today many Westerners (although, regretfully, probably not *most* Westerners) have abandoned notions of Western intellectual, moral, and cultural superiority. A century ago, however, that notion was so widespread that no writer or speaker would have to conceal his or her ethnocentrism.

To Friedrich Fabri, the struggle climaxing in 1871 to create the German nation left the new nation with a kind of postpartum emptiness. Hence, although Fabri does mention the economic benefits of colonialism, he places far more emphasis on German imperialism as a substitute for the once-powerful unifying force of nation creation. Imperialism is, to Fabri, a powerful unifying and "liberating" force that Germany needs in order to achieve true greatness. That force, Fabri writes, must involve the spread of the German culture—an activity he refers to as a "mission" on two occasions in the selection. This, he says, is how Great Britain has achieved primacy: by avoiding destructive wars against other European powers and by reaching outward in a unified fashion for colonies, wealth, and prestige.

Missionary John Paton's letter to James Service will present no basic difficulties for students, for Paton makes a list of the reasons why Great Britain ought to embrace one particular colonial venture, that of taking possession of the New Hebrides. But you may have to help your students identify what Paton considered to be the *most important* reasons. Because of his background, one suspects that points 1 through 7 were arguments Paton thought the British authorities would find appealing, but that they were not of central importance to Paton himself. Protecting missionaries (like himself) and putting an end to blackbirding activities (which made missionary work more difficult and dangerous) were Paton's most important concerns. Ask your students why Paton even bothered to mention points 1 through 7.

Jules Ferry recognized that an industrialized nation would be able to produce manufactured goods faster than the citizens of that nation could consume them. Therefore, if most of the Western nations were industrialized, surpluses of manufactured goods would exist in all those nations, and tariff walls would be erected to shield consumers from foreign goods (which would create even more surpluses). To Ferry, France's only answer to this problem is to establish French colonies that consume French surpluses. Note also the sense of urgency at the end of the selection: if other nations gobble up these territories, where will France send its surpluses?

Addressing a meeting of the West Birmingham Relief Association, Chamberlain produced arguments quite similar to those of Ferry. Chamberlain, however, was speaking to a group of factory workers, many of them doubtless unemployed (as indicated by the name of the association). His emphasis, therefore, was different. As demonstrated by the group's reaction, his was a message they wanted to hear. Although Chamberlain made a few bows to the impulses of "Christianizing" and "civilizing" the host populations, it is obvious from the audience's reaction that these arguments carried considerably less weight than the economic ones. We know from other sources that his real motive was increased markets, and Chamberlain clearly grasped the extent to which his listeners shared his feelings. As for his view of the host populations, Finley Peter Dunne has probably summed up Chamberlain's attitudes in the remarks by his "Mr. Dooley" quoted earlier—though without Chamberlain specifically in mind as the target of the satire.

Ferdinando Martini's argument is as straightforward as those of Fabri, Ferry, and Chamberlain. To achieve national greatness, he declared, Italy must find a way to deal with its serious problem of overpopulation and to stop the hemorrhaging of its human resources to other lands. Note how Martini compared the lives of Ethiopians favorably with those of Italians living in the Campagna (a region of about 800 square miles surrounding Rome) and Basilicata (in southern Italy, northwest of the Gulf of Taranto). Whereas other advocates of imperialism tended to denigrate the host populations, Martini cleverly turned the tables by arguing that these "unfit" peoples actually lived better than Italians. This must have seemed a powerful argument indeed.

Clever journalist G. W. Steevens, with his purple prose, begins by trying to disarm those anti-imperialists who argued that imperialism's costs would never be outweighed by its economic benefits. Steevens agrees totally; his allusion to "a nation of shopkeepers" should be pointed out to students, lest they miss it. Yet his selection is filled with terms like "national redemption," "vindication," "self-respect," and "honor." Make sure your students appreciate that Steevens is less concerned with how others perceive the British than with how the British perceive themselves. A good synonym for his central motive would be "national pride," not terribly different from the principal argument made by Fabri. Yet historical circumstances made Fabri's and Steevens's points different: Germany was a victorious new nation, whereas Great Britain was rebuilding pride after the humiliating loss of Gordon. Thus Kitchener's expedition was not (in Steevens's mind) to destroy the Mahdi and return the Sudan to Egypt (note his opinion of Egyptians), but rather to restore a sense of national pride to the British back home.

To be sure, the evidence does not present all the arguments employed by the imperialists. It does, however, reveal the principal lines of reasoning. Moreover, these selections allow students to see that imperialists in each of these western European nations made use of arguments that were tailored to that nation's own political and economic situation.

Questions to Consider

As with other chapters, this section is intended to sharpen students' thinking about the evidence by posing questions that will lead them through the evidence and serve as a self-test on their comprehension. You can also use these questions for class discussion, blending in the chapter's content goals along with some broader questions (either those we have found effective or others of your own devising).

The most difficult task here will be helping the students stand back and look at the evidence as a whole. The common ground shared by all the advocates is as important to identify as the individual position of each advocate and his special appeal. One way to determine the points in common is to examine the portrayals of the host populations and of the anti-imperialists. From there, students can approach the ways in which the advocates saw the West versus the non-West and their shared belief that the West would benefit from colonialism. Thus, you will have to work "both sides of the street," helping students to understand how each advocate appealed to the specific problems of his own country and, at the same time, how Western imperialism shared common themes. This will be a real challenge.

Finally, a word of caution: do not allow the students to imitate Mr. Dooley—that is, to mock the advocates of imperialism without attempting to understand them. Here the larger questions noted earlier regarding the persistence of beliefs and ideology may uncover student attitudes not so very different from those of Fabri, Paton, Ferry, Chamberlain, Martini, and Steevens.

Epilogue and Evaluation

In addition to fleshing out the story of Western imperialism and suggesting its role in the coming of World War I, the epilogue presents the dilemma that faced host populations. In their efforts to modernize their nations, the peoples of the non-West embraced and came to rely heavily on Western technology. Furthermore, Western political ideology proved to be extremely attractive to those elements seeking to throw off tradition and to ground their political systems in popular participation and the rule of law. At the same time, however, these same elements sought political independence from their colonial masters. Indeed, the West had intruded itself into the non-West in numerous ways, some of which were welcomed by non-Westerners and some abhorred.

Numerous ways of evaluating students' work in this chapter have proved both successful and stimulating. You may want to ask students to write a newspaper account of one (or all) of the selections, noting the speaker's background, the problems faced by his audience, the audience itself, the nature of the appeal, and an evaluation of the speech or writing.

For those of us already awash in student papers, a nonwritten exercise may prove a relief as well as a valuable activity. If video equipment is available, students could be asked to recreate on videotape one of the speeches provided in the chapter, much in the spirit of the "You Are There" television series of the 1950s. A group of students could produce this show, with one student playing the speaker (or writer), one an audience member, one an anti-imperialist critic, and so on. The nonparticipating students could be asked to evaluate the effort. Lacking such technology, students could be asked to present their production "live" before the rest of the class. Make sure that students attempt to recreate a late-nineteenth-century perspective rather than argue from their own late-twentieth-century point of view.

Of course, dividing the class into two groups (imperialists and anti-imperialists) or three groups (imperialists, anti-imperialists, and host populations) is always a good exercise. If you like, you may divide your students into six groups (one for each selection), asking each group to analyze the piece of evidence and to answer the central questions. Whatever form of evaluation you use, you will find that students display a great deal of energy (as they put it) "getting into" the evidence of this chapter.

For Further Reading

Winfried Baumgart, *Imperialism: The Idea and Reality of British and French Colonial Expansion, 1880–1914* (1982). A very good and well-balanced study, which includes a fine chapter on British and French advocates of imperialism.

Raymond Betts, *Europe Overseas: Phases of Imperialism* (1968). Argues that power politics was the most important stimulus to colonization. See also his *The False Dawn: European Imperialism in the Nineteenth Century* (1975), which concludes that empires fulfilled few of their advocates' promises.

Henri Brunschwig, *French Colonialism, 1871–1914: Myths and Realities* (1964). Compares British and French imperialism, asserting that the British were motivated by economic reasons and the French by nationalist fever.

D. K. Fieldhouse, *Economics and Empire, 1830–1914* (1973). Argues that Europe's economic problems did not make imperialism either necessary or inevitable. See also his *Colonialism, 1870–1945* (1981), which claims that many of the arguments for imperialism were designed to justify colonialism to the electorate.

Heinz Gollwitzer, *Europe in the Age of Imperialism, 1880–1914* (1969). A competent overview of parallel economic, demographic, technological, and social trends in Europe.

Daniel R. Headrick, *The Tentacles of Progress: Technology Transfer in the Age of Imperialism, 1850–1940* (1988). Excellent study of the benefits and liabilities of bringing Western technology to host populations.

E. J. Hobsbawm, *The Age of Empire, 1875–1914* (1987). An excellent comprehensive study.

John M. Mackenzie (ed.), *Imperialism and Popular Culture* (1986). A first-rate, imaginative study of how popular culture advocated imperialism in Great Britain.

CHAPTER TEN
To the Age Its Art, 1870–1920

Chapter 10 is the final exercise in "traditional" intellectual history in Volume II of *Discovering the Western Past*. Its approach to the history of Western thought is far different, however, from that of Chapters 3 and 7, which relied exclusively on printed sources. Here we present the student with another source for intellectual history, the art of an era. Our objective here, as in all the chapters of *Discovering the Western Past*, is to acquaint students with the full range of sources that historians can draw on in reconstructing the past. Through the medium of modern art, we propose to introduce students to many of the intellectual problems of our modern age, problems that often still vex Western society.

The Problem

Content objectives:

1. to understand in general terms the major developments in physical and social sciences

2. to measure the impact on modern Western thought of such scientific breakthroughs as Darwin's evolution theory and Einstein's relativity theory

3. to measure the impact on Western thought of other developments and historical events, including World War I

Skills objectives:

1. to analyze the art of the late nineteenth and early twentieth centuries to determine how it reflected sweeping scientific and existential changes in the Western experience

2. to use the findings of this analysis to draw general conclusions about the development of modern thought

Sources and Method

Most Western Civilization textbooks include some mention of art; but with the need to accomplish their manifold goals of presenting a political, social, and intellectual framework for understanding the history of the West, few books can devote extensive attention to this subject. Some even restrict their treatment of art to the inclusion, with little or no comment, of a section of photographs.

   The student using such a textbook confronts a serious gap in coverage, because art reflects the world view of the age that produces it. The reward for students in analyzing modern art is a better understanding of modern thought. We have selected the years between 1870 and 1920 because they represent a period of particular ferment, one in which developments in the physical and social sciences challenged traditional Western patterns of thought. We have devoted an unusually long background section in this chapter to the general trends in late-nineteenth- and early-twentieth-century thought because we believe that such information is essential for students to interpret modern art successfully.

   This chapter may be used in its chronological context of the late nineteenth and early twentieth centuries, or you may wish to combine it with Chapters 3 and 7 to form an intellectual history unit in your course. All three chapters deal with a single aspect of the Enlightenment, the key event in Western thought after the Renaissance: Chapter 3 presents the Enlightenment faith in science; Chapter 7 traces the political application of Enlightenment ideals in nineteenth-century liberalism and socialism; and Chapter 10 offers the modern counterchallenge to Enlightenment ideals. However you employ this chapter, students should derive from it basic skills in understanding the history of thought.

The Evidence

In our experience, this chapter poses the greatest challenge of the three intellectual history chapters in Volume II of *Discovering the Western Past*. *Students* find this chapter difficult for a number of reasons. Most leave secondary school with little background in art history or the interpretation of art. Moreover, many receive their first systematic introduction to Western thought, the larger topic within which this chapter interprets art, only in the Western Civilization course for which we designed *Discovering the Western Past*. This material, therefore, is virtually brand new to many students.

Understanding the importance of the ideas that this chapter's evidence represents is critical to students' success in interpretation. Once they understand the pivotal nature of the thought characteristic of the period 1870 to 1920, we have found them much better prepared to analyze the art of Chapter 10. Accordingly, we have provided a detailed Problem section in this chapter. You may even wish to amplify this section in class discussion, pointing out, perhaps, that developments in the physical and social sciences between 1870 and 1920 continue to define the way we look at ourselves and our world.

Once they become aware of the significance of the developments in late-nineteenth- and early-twentieth-century thought, students should find the arrangement of the evidence interesting. We have limited the subject of the works of art that we selected for inclusion: all are portrayals of the human form. We have ordered these paintings to reflect their creators' progressively widening break with the artistic conventions of their age. And we have provided central questions for this chapter that require students to trace that growing divergence from tradition and to relate it to the intellectual life of the late-nineteenth- and early-twentieth-century West.

We have had particular success in directing students' analysis and discussion of these sources by analyzing a few of the sources in class. We always emphasize Sources 1 and 2, the works by the neoclassicist Ingres and the romantic Delacroix. Students should have no problem in recognizing differences in the two artists' interpretive styles. What may be harder for them to recognize is the fact that the two works, however different, embody the same nineteenth-century artistic convention: the effort to paint an almost photographlike representation of the human form. Ask students to study closely the persons portrayed in these paintings in order to understand the basic similarities of their creators' styles. Gaining an awareness of what was "conventional" for nineteenth-century art audiences will provide students with a foundation for appreciating the revolutionary nature of artistic deviation from that convention.

With the art of Seurat, van Gogh, Gauguin, Rousseau, and Munch (Sources 3 through 7), students confront a greater challenge to their analytical skills. We successfully present this material, however, by analyzing one work with students to show them how to use the background material in the Sources and Method section. We link Seurat's *La Grande Jatte*, for example, to the attempt to study color and form in a "scientific" manner that grew out of nineteenth-century advances in scientific knowledge.

Sources 8 through 11 fulfill most laypersons' stereotypes of "incomprehensible" modern art. We have found that this group of paintings initially offers students the greatest challenge of all. Again, we often guide their efforts by drawing on background information in analyzing a single work as an example. Students' individual study of the other paintings in this group should result in a clear understanding of the deep upheaval and transformation of all intellectual conventions in the late nineteenth and early twentieth centuries.

Questions to Consider

This section asks students to draw some fairly sophisticated conclusions from the paintings that constitute the evidence in Chapter 10. With the chapter's background material, the leading questions in the Questions to Consider section, and perhaps a bit more guidance from the instructor, students can successfully complete their analysis of the paintings.

We designed the intellectual history chapters of *Discovering the Western Past* to present varied and increasingly sophisticated problems in the history of Western thought. As students complete the analysis in Chapter 10, we like to pose still broader questions, leading them to consider the intellectual history of the West as a whole from the Enlightenment to the twentieth century. We ask them such questions as: What is the changing vision of humankind over the two centuries we have studied? What has become of Alexander Pope's optimistic faith and the belief held by both Tocqueville and Marx that the world could be explained in rational terms? Why has this transformation occurred? How have developments during the middle and late twentieth century, especially in the sciences, affected Western thought? Questions such as these in classroom discussion can draw trends in intellectual history together for your students.

Epilogue and Evaluation

Our epilogue takes students beyond 1920 in Western art, suggesting how they can continue to apply the analytical skills they developed in this chapter. We sometimes present slides of late-twentieth-century painting in class to demonstrate the nature of that art and also to evaluate student mastery of this chapter's material. We have, for example, asked students to look at the abstract expressionism of Jackson Pollock, assessing their analysis of his work and that of other modern artists.

More conventional evaluation can take the form of a writing project that might be phrased as follows: In the late nineteenth century, the Enlightenment's faith in human rationality and in people's ability to achieve positive material progress came under serious attack. What developments constituted this attack? How was it reflected in the art of the late nineteenth and early twentieth centuries?

For Further Reading

H. H. Arnason, *History of Modern Art: Painting, Sculpture, Architecture* (1968). A copiously illustrated survey of modern art.

Wolf Dieter Dube, *The Expressionists* (1972). A useful treatment of this important movement in modern art.

H. W. Janson, *History of Art: A Survey of the Major Visual Arts from the Dawn of History to the Present Day* (1962 and later editions). This fine work endures as the premiere survey of art history.

John Rewald, *The History of Impressionism* (1961) and *Post-Impressionism from Van Gogh to Gauguin* (1962). Highly reliable treatments of their subjects published by the Museum of Modern Art in New York.

Hans Richter, *Dada: Art and Anti-Art* (1978). A treatment of the Dada movement by a participant.

Robert Rosenblum, *Cubism and Twentieth-Century Art* (1976). A good study of cubism.

Carl E. Schorske, *Fin-de-siècle Vienna: Politics and Culture* (1981). A study of Viennese culture with an important discussion of Klimt and his artistic milieu.

Roland N. Stromberg, *European Intellectual History Since 1789* (1981). This excellent work remains the best survey to date of modern European intellectual history.

CHAPTER ELEVEN

World War I: Total War

Participants called it the "Great War." Woodrow Wilson optimistically hoped it would be "the war to end all wars." By 1918 every Western adult appreciated the gravity of the conflict Europeans had embarked on so enthusiastically in August 1914. Our goal in this chapter is to convey to late-twentieth-century students the impact of a combat among nations that was the first total war, an initiation for the West into the horrors of modern warfare.

In this chapter we draw on a variety of sources to present the war to students while illustrating the range of primary materials available to historians. The types of evidence introduced to students for the first time in Chapter 11 include works of poetry and fiction composed by World War I combatants. More familiar evidence includes a memoir, letters, a government report, and statistical data.

The Problem

Content objectives:

1. to learn the nature of the techniques of war introduced in World War I

2. to assess the impact of this kind of armed combat on both individuals and their nations

3. to understand how World War I shaped events after the 1918 armistice

Skills objectives:

1. to analyze modern poetry and prose for the historical insights these literary forms contain

2. to combine literary analysis with study of more conventional historical sources to assess the nature and impact of World War I

Sources and Method

Our aim in this chapter is to convey to students the all-encompassing nature of modern combat unleashed for the first time in World War I. To achieve this goal we have assembled sources from three of the major European belligerents: England, France, and Germany. We have chosen sources that introduce students to both the front line and the home front in the war, and we have arranged the evidence to allow students to examine and assess the cumulative effect of the conflict on its participants.

The Problem section describes briefly for students the impact of the war on the battle and home fronts. We use a number of classroom techniques to enhance students' understanding of both phases of the war. We always emphasize for students the new firepower available to armies by 1914, a firepower whose effects on the conduct of war were not completely understood because Europe had not witnessed a general war in about a century. Nothing better reveals that tragic misunderstanding than the casualty rates of the war's early days. France suffered the greatest losses of all the major powers (see Source 14), and this figure serves as our example. French army sources show that between its entry into the war on August 3 and the end of that month, France suffered 206,515 casualties (dead, wounded, or missing soldiers) out of 1,600,000 men in uniform.

Our sources indicate the cost of the war on the home front in terms of casualties suffered through bombings, reduced rations, and sagging morale, and they also suggest sweeping social and economic changes that would result from women's war efforts and wartime indebtedness. We amplify these sources by pointing to other costs of the war. For example, individual liberties and even parliamentary government also were among the war's casualties. The Defense of the Realm Act circumscribed civilian rights in Britain; in France the Clemenceau ministry summarily arrested journalists and politicians critical of the war effort in 1917 and 1918. In Germany the war produced a virtual military dictatorship by 1918. The war affected every aspect of life in the belligerent nations.

The Evidence

We have tested all the sources in this chapter with Western Civilization classes, and we have found a remarkably high level of student interest in the Great War. That interest is sustained even as the students read what will be the most challenging of this chapter's evidence, Sources 1, 2, 3, 6, and 7. These selections are all poems and thus represent a literary form many students approach with some reluctance.

To encourage students in their analysis of these poems, we have provided considerable detail on the authors. As the Sources and Méthod section suggests, students should be guided to identify the central message of each poem. We generally read aloud and analyze Rupert Brooke's poem (Source 1), one of the more difficult selections, to demonstrate analytical techniques to students. But even without benefit of this exercise students should have little trouble with the other poetry, which indeed can stand alone. The poems of Brooke, Péguy, and Lissauer (Sources 1 through 3) clearly demonstrate the early enthusiasm for the war. The poems of Owen and Sassoon (Sources 6 and 7) reveal the war's devastating effects on the authors during service in the trenches.

We include selections from Henri Barbusse's *Under Fire* (Source 4) and Erich Maria Remarque's *All Quiet on the Western Front* (Source 5) that lend vivid detail to the sentiments expressed by the poets Owen and Sassoon. Letters from German soldiers (Sources 8 and 9) also should show students that patriotic fervor was one of the war's first casualties as the reality of modern combat bore down on soldiers of all the warring nations.

The home front offers many possibilities for class discussion. Women's history may be addressed through the memoirs of Vera Brittain (Source 10) and the statistical summary of female wartime employment in England (Source 13). We think it is important to emphasize female participation in the war effort because it played an essential role in the subsequent enfranchisement of women in many nations at the war's end. Some attention to women's history at this juncture also provides a convenient transition to Chapter 12, which we devote entirely to women's history.

The cost of war on the home front can be measured in the U.S. Army's analysis of German rations at the war's end (Source 11). If German diet suffered because of the war, so did civilian morale in every country. The report of the Prefect of the Isère is graphic proof of French morale problems (Source 12). You may wish to heighten students' awareness of the crisis atmosphere in which this report was written by emphasizing that 1917 was the year of disaster for the Allied side: France's army mutinied; German submarine warfare brought England to the brink of starvation until the United States entered the war in April 1917; the Italian armies collapsed at Caporetto; and the Bolshevik Revolution drove Russia from the war. Hence, the concern of the French government for civilian morale was justified.

The war had other costs, too. Source 15 suggests the economic cost in terms of Allied indebtedness to America. But the ultimate cost of the war was in lives lost. Source 14 is a clear accounting of the estimated war dead. Students worked with statistical evidence early in *Discovering the Western Past,* and they should easily assimilate the significance of the data in Source 14. You may, however, wish to direct their attention to the last three columns, the per capita losses that tell the most about the war's price for each nation. In class discussion we sometimes recall Churchill's assessment of the war's cost from *The World Crisis:* "Victory was to be bought as dear as to be almost indistinguishable from defeat."

Questions to Consider

In this section we pose a number of questions intended to guide students in answering the chapter's central questions. But you may wish to present additional questions for classroom discussion. We find particularly useful those that direct students beyond the second decade of the twentieth century toward an understanding of the long-range effects of the war. You might ask such questions as: Why did every defeated country experience a revolution in 1918 or 1919? What sort of resentments would wartime sacrifices have bred in defeated countries? What fundamental economic changes might result from vast Allied indebtedness to the United States? Why might French politicians in the 1930s hesitate to confront a resurgent Germany if the price was war?

Epilogue and Evaluation

The intent of our epilogue is to guide students toward an understanding of the events of the 1930s leading to World War II. The rise of Hitler, appeasement, and ultimately the European outbreak of war in 1939 are impossible to put in context without a broad understanding of the impact of World War I.

Besides textbook and lecture material relating to World War I, we have successfully used a role-playing device to evaluate student mastery of this chapter's sources. We divide the class into national "delegations" to the Paris peace conference, and we provide them with some background information on the personalities of the leaders of each of the delegations: the American Woodrow Wilson, whom the French found a trifle sanctimonious (Clemenceau is alleged to have said of Wilson's Fourteen Points that God Almighty only needed ten points!); the British prime minister David Lloyd George, who had just won reelection by promising to "Hang the Kaiser"; the French prime minister Georges Clemenceau, the "Tiger of France," who, on taking office in 1917, was asked in the Chamber of Deputies what his policy would be and replied directly, "I make war"; Vittorio Orlando, who led a divided Italian government; and the Social Democrats who represented a defeated Germany in the midst of domestic political turmoil. Then we ask students to present the arguments of their "country" for shaping the peace settlement. The ensuing exchange will provide instructors with ample evidence of the level of student understanding of World War I. More traditional writing assignments also can be based on this chapter.

For Further Reading

Jean-Jacques Becker, *The Great War and the French People*, trans. Arnold Pomerans (1986). A good study of the war's impact on France.

Bernard Bergonzi, *Heroes' Twilight: A Study of the Literature of the Great War* (1965). A major study of English poetry, novels, and autobiographies describing the war.

Paul Fussell, *The Great War and Modern Memory* (1975). A second important study of the war's impact on English literature.

L. F. Haber, *The Poisonous Cloud: Chemical Warfare in the First World War* (1986). A recent study of the poisonous gas used by both sides in the war.

P. E. Hager and D. Taylor (eds.), *The Novels of World War I: An Annotated Bibliography* (1981). A complete guide to the fiction produced by the war experience in all major European languages.

Alistair Horne, *The Price of Glory: Verdun, 1916* (1967). A dramatic account of one of the war's greatest battles.

Martin Middlebrook, *The First Day of the Somme* (1971) and *The Kaiser's Battle, 21 March 1918: The First Day of the German Spring Offensive* (1978). These two books draw on the experiences of soldiers involved in the battles to present excellent accounts of some of the costliest fighting on the Western Front.

Bernadotte E. Schmitt and Harold C. Vedeler, *The World in the Crucible, 1914–1919* (1984). A recent comprehensive history of the war.

Roland Stromberg, *Redemption by War: The Intellectuals and 1914* (1982). A study of how and why the intellectuals of all European countries initially welcomed the war.

R. M. Watt, *Dare Call It Treason* (1963). A good treatment of one of the war's most dramatic events, the mutiny of the French army in 1917.

Trevor Wilson, *The Myriad Faces of War: Britain and the Great War, 1914–1918* (1968). A comprehensive study of the British war effort, at home and at the front.

Denis Winter, *Death's Men: Soldiers of the Great War* (1978). A study of the fighting conditions endured by British soldiers.

J. M. Winter, *The Great War and the British People* (1986). A modern study of the war's impact on Britain.

Robert Wohl, *The Generation of 1914* (1979). A remarkable comparative study of the war's intellectual impact in France, Germany, England, Italy, and Spain.

CHAPTER TWELVE

Women in Russian Revolutionary Movements

In response to the tremendous upsurge of interest in women's history and the resulting vast amount of new research, most Western Civilization textbooks now include some material on women. This is a welcome change, but unfortunately most of the discussion occurs within the context of two topics—the family and the women's rights movement—causing students to absorb two misperceptions about the historical experience of women. The first misperception is that the family was always the most important determinant of women's experience, making women's history and family history essentially the same thing. (Regrettably this view is also held by many historians, particularly those whose research has never involved either women or the family.) The second misperception is that women rarely played a role in major historical movements other than those specifically concerned with the position of women. This chapter attempts to counter both these false views with a striking example of women's actions set totally outside the context of the family; the sources represented here show women participating in events that shaped one of the world's great powers.

There is yet another reason for the focus of this chapter. Research in the history of women during many eras has revealed not only how women's experience was ignored and devalued—it was not deemed "history"—but also how the historical record was consciously altered to leave out women's contributions. The story of the Russian Revolution provides one of the more blatant examples of this practice. Students are thus quite easily able to discover for themselves the gender bias of the historical record and to consider the types of sources and information that could be used to correct this bias.

The Problem

Content objectives:

1. to learn about the aims and actions of a wide variety of groups pushing for change in tsarist Russia

2. to examine the role of women within these groups

3. to identify those problems that various segments of Russian society viewed as most important

4. to observe the role of class in determining the ideology and membership of Russian revolutionary movements

Skills objectives:

1. to assess the role of gender in shaping human experience

2. to trace change over time and evaluate the reasons for that change

3. to observe how subsequent events can influence an individual's memories and thus his or her written record of an experience

By asking students to consider how they would rewrite their textbooks after working through this chapter, we have intentionally opened the door to a much broader discussion of the ways in which history can be rewritten to include women. (You could widen this discussion still further by talking about other groups that have been left out of the historical record and ways of including them.) One way to approach this topic is to think about what a timeline of "great events in women's history" would look like. Would the Russian Revolution be included? The American? The Industrial? If many events commonly featured on historical timelines were left out, what new information would be added? Women's suffrage? The development of the birth control pill? The vulcanization of rubber, which allowed for the invention of the baby bottle nipple, leading to the end of wet nursing?

The tendency among the Soviets to rewrite their own history has recently received a great deal of coverage in the American press, with the end of the Soviet Union and Gorbachev's and Yeltsin's vows to tell the true story at last. Because a central issue of this chapter is what gets left out when history is written and rewritten, it may be interesting to have your students speculate on whether the women's actions they are reading about may finally enter official Soviet history. Gorbachev and Yeltsin have made public a number of historical events that had been neglected or ignored, such as the horrific results of the collectivization of agriculture and the harsh treatment some national minorities received during Stalin's attempts to break nationalist consciousness, but they have not, to our knowledge, mentioned the male bias of the official view of the past. This omission could provide a good example both of the pervasiveness of gender bias in writing history and of the continued male domination of Russian society.

Sources and Method

In terms of method, this chapter is one of the simplest in either volume of *Discovering the Western Past* because the basic technique for analyzing the sources is simply careful reading, an ability that seemed too self-evident and universal for us to include in our "skills objectives" list. In terms of analysis, however, this chapter is one of the most sophisticated because it asks students to consider the intersection of class and gender as determinants of human experience, a subject many historians back away from as too complex or difficult.

Before you provide a factual or contextual background, you may need to discuss exactly how historians use the concepts "class" and "gender." We have discovered that many U.S. undergraduates are familiar with the economic divisions of upper, middle, and lower class but are entirely unfamiliar with the notion of "working class" or "proletariat." To them, "working class" sounds pejorative; almost all describe themselves as members of the middle class no matter what their parents' occupation or family income. You may have confronted this issue already in your discussions of industrialization, but it is important to stress again here that "working class" is not synonymous with "peasantry" and that an individual's class status was not simply a matter of economics during the period discussed here. If this is the first time you have talked about the idea of class, you will probably need to emphasize that viewing society as comprised of classes does not automatically make one a Marxist, and that people in capitalist countries like Britain and Germany also think of themselves or describe others as "working class." (Why "working class" has disappeared as a common term in American political discussions is an interesting issue, but one that would be hard to integrate with the material in this chapter; perhaps it could be examined at some point if you discuss contemporary American popular mythology.)

If "class" is a concept foreign to your students, "gender" may be even more unfamiliar. We provide a simple definition of this term in the text ("what it means cognitively to be male or female"), and you may wish to discuss further the differences between the terms "sex" and "gender." (On the other hand, this may be a topic you wish to avoid because it can lead to some heated arguments that bear only slightly on the Russian Revolution.) Once your students have assessed the discussion of women in their textbooks, they may also wish to qualify our rather optimistic statement that "sophisticated analysts of any historical change now investigate the differing roles played by men and women." Or they may wish to return to the distinctions between ideal, idealization, and reality made in Chapter 2 of Volume I, recognizing that this statement is most probably our own idealization of the true state of affairs.

Western Civilization textbooks show tremendous variation in their coverage of the nineteenth-century women's rights movement. Some discuss it quite thoroughly; some mention it briefly as one of many reform movements during the nineteenth century; and several we have looked at devote as little as one sentence to the topic. For this reason the amount of background you will have to provide depends on the text you have chosen. The same holds true for reform movements in Russia. The Russian Revolution itself generally receives a thorough treatment, but the wide assortment of groups who played a role are often reduced to three: Kerensky's moderates, the Mensheviks, and the Bolsheviks. Because many of the women whose words provide the evidence in this chapter belonged to other, smaller groups, you may need to discuss some of them and their aims a bit more fully.

Although there were disagreements among the various reform and revolutionary groups on every conceivable subject, some of these disputes were more important than others, and you may wish to identify them before your students read the sources. Key points of disagreement include: whether force should be used to bring about social change and, if so, whether it should be directed against persons or only against property; whether a revolution should depend on the workers, as Marx suggested, or whether the peasant class could also be mobilized into an active force; whether change should come only from grassroots demands or from a small group of leaders; and whether it was necessary for intellectuals to experience the life of peasants or workers in order to understand their problems. Many of the authors in this chapter stated their own positions on these matters or attempted to put their beliefs into action by working in factories or organizing peasants. It is important that your students realize that these women were not alone in their concern about such things. The women revolutionaries in this chapter stood not on the fringes but directly in the center of their various groups.

The Evidence

Sources 1 through 4 are all personal memoirs, written after the events they describe. In relation to Saint-Simon in Chapter 2, you have probably already discussed how historians use memoirs as a source; but you may wish to refresh your students' memories on that subject here, emphasizing such points as objectivity, the perspective provided by hindsight, and the sense of self, and noting the differences between memoirs and diaries. These issues may be discussed generally; or you may examine them simply in the context of this chapter by having your students consider whether the three memoirs that were published after the Bolshevik Revolution (Sources 1, 3, and 4) differ significantly from the one published before (Source 2). Do those published in Moscow (Sources 1 through 3) differ in tone from Broido's account (Source 4), which was first published in Berlin after she was forced into exile? Though you have doubtless discussed earlier in the course why we need to pay attention to the date and place of publication of primary and secondary sources, this would be the natural place to bring up the matter again. (We have mentioned these issues explicitly at the beginning of the Questions to Consider section.)

The two petitions (Sources 6 and 7) are straightforward and should not require much additional background, but you may wish to say something more about Alexandra Kollontai, the author of Sources 5, 8, and 9. We have mentioned that she was the only important woman among the Soviet leadership (except for Lenin's wife, who still played primarily a supporting role), and you may wish to stress this fact even further, especially in considering the uniqueness of her ideas and the failure of most of them to be implemented. Kollontai is a fascinating figure because she recognizes the distinctive problems of women (she makes what we would term a feminist analysis of the situation), yet she tries to view society completely from the perspective of class. Indeed, Kollontai's experience provides one of the earliest examples of the difficulty of trying to fit the issue of women into a class analysis; the cool response of her associates is likewise an early example of the hostility to feminism among doctrinaire Marxists. As the British scholar Heide Hartman succinctly put it, "The marriage of Marxism and feminism has been like the marriage of husband and wife in English common law: Marxism and feminism are one, and that one is Marxism."

Questions to Consider

This section asks students to consider the roles of three key historical variables: time, class, and gender. Though it is somewhat dangerous to generalize about the course of revolutionary movements in Russia because each was strikingly different, most historians would agree that these movements grew gradually more willing to use violence and became increasingly certain that a revolution, not mere reform, was needed. Successive acts of repression by the tsarist government led to the opposite of their intended result by convincing increasingly more people of the validity of the revolutionaries' goals.

Your students will probably have been struck by the fact that practically all the authors came from the middle class or intelligentsia, even though they identified with and attempted to enlist the support of the working class and in some cases the peasants. This was true, of course, of male revolutionaries in Russia as well, but the women's sense of empathy with the poor and the peasantry appears stronger than that of their male colleagues. Perhaps their experiences of oppression and exclusion because of their gender made them better able to understand class oppression, or perhaps they were simply more willing to describe subjective attitudes because such language was more acceptable coming from a woman.

Some of your students may point out that the second main question, which asks them to compare the experiences of women and men, is difficult to answer because we have not included any sources written by men. We debated including some sources from male authors but decided against it for three reasons, any of which you may wish to point out and discuss further in class. The first was simply lack of space, because we wanted to impress on the reader the tremendous variety of female experience; including works by men would have made our point, that it is difficult to generalize about all women, less forceful. Second, most of the women comment extensively about the ideas and actions of their male associates, thus giving the reader an opportunity for comparison; similar pieces by men almost never discuss how their ideas differ from those of the women who worked with them, nor do they mention women's ideas at all. The third reason is related to this last point. For centuries the male experience has been defined as the "human" experience, and the story of women, when it is told at all, is derived totally from the words of men. This chapter reverses the tradition; if students comment that they cannot really know anything about the ideas of men from only the writings of women, an obvious response is: What do we know about the ideas of women from the writings of men—which constitute the vast majority of historical sources?

Epilogue and Evaluation

The epilogue traces both the fates of the nineteenth-century revolutionaries and the changing status of women after the Bolshevik Revolution. This may be a good opportunity to stress again the distinction between ideal and reality that we have drawn in so many chapters. In theory, women have total equality in Russia; in reality, that "equality" means they generally work the same hours as men outside the home and then perform all the domestic tasks as well. Many of the professions in which Russian women far outnumber their American counterparts—medicine and engineering, for example—do not carry the high status and corresponding high salary that they do in the

United States. (This circumstance is, of course, intimately related to the large percentage of women in such professions in Russia. One of the constants of women's history in every culture and at every time is a drop in status and salary whenever women enter an occupation; this effect has been traced most clearly in the United States in the cases of teachers, secretaries, and telephone operators.)

Along with evaluating class discussion or a writing assignment, the best way to assess students' mastery of the chapter's main analytical point may be to ask them to attempt the assignment suggested at the end of the Questions to Consider section—namely, to rewrite the portion of their text that discusses Russian revolutionary movements, incorporating what they have now learned about women. Or students could be assigned other parts of the text to rewrite, or at least to investigate, in terms of the lack of inclusion of women's contributions. Are women mentioned in discussions of the rise of nineteenth-century western European socialism? The pacifist movement after World War I? The nineteenth-century social reform movements for child labor laws, an end to prostitution, and temperance? In the context of temperance, are they presented primarily as saloon smashers or as serious legislative petitioners? Is the fact that women invented the public opinion poll mentioned in the text? These are only a few topics your students could tackle. If rewriting the text is too long a task, you could simply ask them to compile a list of sources that would enable them to make a start at integrating the experiences of women. Some students may have difficulty finding any sources at all, and their dilemma would reinforce the point that it is much more difficult for the historian to discover the female experience than the male.

For Further Reading

Dorothy Atkinson, Alexander Dallin, and Gail Warshofsky Lapidus (eds.), *Women in Russia* (1977). A collection of articles covering many aspects of women's life in the Soviet Union.

Linda Edmondson, *Feminism in Russia, 1900–1917* (1984). Examines the middle-class feminist movement in the period immediately preceding the Russian Revolution, noting the previously unacknowledged influence of feminists on the plans and goals of other groups.

Vera Figner, *Memoirs of a Revolutionist* (1968). Good English translation of a very moving account by the most revered of the Russian women revolutionaries.

Gail Warshofsky Lapidus, *Women in Soviet Society: Equality, Development and Social Change* (1978). Sets the status of Soviet women in historical perspective, using statistical evidence.

Richard Stites, *The Women's Liberation Movement in Russia: Feminism, Nihilism, and Bolshevism 1860–1930* (1978). Explores the often conflicting aims and allegiances of radical Russian women.

Franco Venturi, *Roots of Revolution: A History of the Populist and Socialist Movements in Nineteenth Century Russia* (1964). An extremely thorough discussion of the wide variety of populist and socialist groups.

CHAPTER THIRTEEN

Selling a Totalitarian System

Recent studies of the Nazis' rise to power have emphasized the extent of the party's support in Germany. Contrary to traditional assumptions, these studies suggest, the Nazis' appeal was not confined to a narrow segment of society, namely, the lower middle classes. Chapter 13 represents our effort to show students how the Nazis mobilized their support; the aim is to give students a deeper understanding of the Nazi rise to power. As Albert Speer suggests in the selection quoted at the opening of Chapter 13, the Nazis were pioneers in the use of modern media to mold public opinion.

The Problem

Content objectives:

1. to understand the changes brought to modern politics by universal suffrage

2. to understand National Socialist ideology

3. to examine how the Nazi party portrayed its ideology to the German voter by means of twentieth-century media techniques

4. to understand the conditions in Germany that made the German public receptive to Nazi manipulation of modern media

Skills objectives:

1. to understand the persuasive powers and potential for misuse of modern political advertising

2. to analyze the techniques of political advertising in order to understand its mass appeal

Sources and Method

Chapter 13 should accomplish two main goals. It should help the student understand the Nazi phenomenon in Germany by analyzing the party's propaganda message. It should further inform the student about the nature of modern mass politics and how media can be used, regardless of ideology, to gain power for a cause.

The Nazis were skilled pioneers in the use of media and political propaganda. Certainly they exploited those post–World War I conditions in Germany we refer to in the epilogue of Chapter 11 and describe here in some detail in the Problem section. But the Nazis also formulated techniques for swaying political opinion that can be applied universally. To reinforce this point, we often turn classroom discussion to a subject very familiar to students: recent U.S. presidential campaigns. Students should have no trouble discerning that victory in recent elections went to the candidates whose advertising presented the clearest and simplest messages. Political disaster seemed to await those candidates whose advertising failed to identify clear and simple themes and "bogged down" in detailed analyses of issues. Of course, one should not discount the importance of the personalities involved in the campaigns and the specific issues that candidates raised. Nevertheless, their use of the media should not be underrated. Then we often shock students by pointing out Hitler's understanding of the use of political propaganda based on a small number of simply stated and constantly repeated issues, as revealed in Source 1. In our experience, no other approach to the subject of Chapter 13 better demonstrates to students the relevance of the chapter's material.

The Evidence

Chapter 13 assembles a variety of evidence to show students how the Nazis successfully mounted their campaign for power. You may reinforce student understanding of this process by briefly outlining the technological and methodological advances on which the National Socialists drew. By the

1930s, modern technology had added the mass circulation newspaper, the radio, the loudspeaker, and the campaign airplane to the potential political arsenal of candidates. The Nazis, unfortunately, were the first to recognize how these breakthroughs could be employed in modern politics, and they also capitalized on new techniques in using media. Chapter 11 should already have shown students the importance of the home front in modern warfare; every belligerent nation in World War I used advertising and propaganda in an attempt to keep its home front united behind the war effort and to sap its enemies' will to fight. Hitler correctly deduced that such techniques could be used to win domestic political support, and Sources 1 and 2 demonstrate his understanding of the matter.

Sources 3 through 16 illustrate the various means by which the Nazis brought their message to the German people. You may wish to emphasize for students that, no matter what the issues, the Nazis addressed them simply and with increasing effectiveness. Goebbels's memorandum (Source 3) and his diary (Source 16) reveal the great effort that went into Nazi advertising. Goebbels's insistence on controlling every detail of party media demonstrates the importance both he and Hitler placed on this area. Goebbels's description of the Hitler poster with the party leader posed against a simple black background shows his skill in these efforts.

The message of much of Nazi advertising and image building remains frightening over five decades later. Students should be encouraged to analyze that message for a thorough understanding of the Nazi phenomenon. Hitler early grasped the role terror could play in moving people's minds (Sources 2 and 15). "Scare tactics" are evident in such evidence as the pamphlet (Source 14) that circulated in Hamburg, stirring up fears of American-style department stores among the German lower middle class, many of whom owned small shops. And the role of fear and prejudice should be readily apparent in Source 8.

Hitler and Goebbels also correctly identified the isolation that the individual often feels in modern industrial society, a sensation heightened by the disorientation many Germans felt as a result of their country's loss of its world power status through defeat in World War I. You may note these phenomena for students to guide them in understanding the appeal of marching men (Source 4) supplied with banners, songs, and slogans (Sources 5, 6, 12) as well as an apparent mass following (Source 11). Clearly the Nazis aimed at tapping the desire of many Germans to "belong." And they portrayed themselves as a party committed to action, deliberately contrasting this attitude with that of the democratic parties, which they characterized as "do nothing" organizations paralyzed in the face of Germany's postwar problems (Sources 7, 13, 15).

The posters in Sources 8 through 10 illustrate aspects of the Nazis' message to aid students in understanding their campaign. Nevertheless, we have found it difficult at times to lead students to an overview of the campaign's effect in Germany. In the light of all we know of Hitler's policies, especially the Holocaust, students find it difficult to comprehend the enthusiasm Hitler's movement succeeded in generating. You may wish to stress the reality of that enthusiasm still more strongly to your students. Sources 17 and 18 describe German fervor for the Nazis in graphic terms and help to explain why success crowned Hitler and Goebbels's efforts.

Questions to Consider

Here we provide highly focused questions designed to lead students to the answers to the main questions of this chapter: Why did the Nazi party appeal to Germans? How did it use modern media to aid its rise to power?

In classroom discussion we especially like to follow up the concluding question of this section, which invites students to compare Nazi methods for amassing political support with those of Louis XIV described in Chapter 2. We have found students to be extremely interested in politics and political techniques. If you pose questions in class discussion obliging them to compare early modern monarchical techniques of rallying support with those of modern political parties in an age of universal suffrage, you should elicit a wide-ranging discussion on the nature of modern politics.

Epilogue and Evaluation

The epilogue takes students beyond the Nazi seizure of power in 1933 to show how propaganda techniques perfected in the years of the party's campaign for power were used to generate support for the Nazi government and the war into which it led Germany.

Your evaluation of student mastery of this chapter can take many forms. We prefer a written assignment that asks students to pull together the material in this chapter and in their textbook to analyze the Nazi phenomenon. Such an assignment might ask, for example, what particular conditions in Germany after World War I favored the rise of a fascist party; what causes the Nazis claimed to stand for; and how modern media promoted their rise to political power.

For Further Reading

William Sheridan Allen, *The Nazi Seizure of Power: The Experience of a Single German Town, 1922–1945*, rev. ed. (1984). A study of the Nazi takeover in one small north German city, this work conveys the tensions of the period, party methodology, and the impact of the takeover far more clearly than most "national" studies of Germany during this period.

Ernest K. Bramsted, *Goebbels and National Socialist Propaganda, 1925–1945* (1965), and Z. A. B. Zeman, Nazi Propaganda (1964). Two reliable general studies of National Socialist propaganda, both focusing on how it was used after Hitler came to power.

Alan Bullock, Hitler: *A Study in Tyranny*, rev. ed. (1964), and Joachim C. Fest, *Hitler* (1973). Excellent studies of the German dictator.

Thomas Childers, *The Nazi Voter: The Social Foundations of Fascism in Germany* (1983), and Richard F. Hamilton, *Who Voted for Hitler?* (1982). Two recent important assessments of the electoral appeal of Nazism that contradict the traditional view that the party's greatest support came from the lower middle class.

Oron J. Hale, *The Captive Press in the Third Reich* (1964). The basic study of Nazi press control after 1933.

Berthold Hinz, *Art in the Third Reich* (1979). A study of the Nazis' post–1933 attempt to employ art in their propaganda message.

Ian Kershaw, *The "Hitler Myth": Image and Reality in the Third Reich* (1987). A thorough study of the development of Hitler's "image" as infallible leader.

David Welch, *Propaganda and the German Cinema, 1933–1945* (1983). A scholarly treatment of the use of film in Nazi propaganda.

CHAPTER FOURTEEN

The Perils of Prosperity: The Unrest of Youth in the 1960s

Modern university students are beneficiaries of the post–World War II prosperity that allowed both communist and noncommunist nations to open higher educational opportunities to their citizens on an unprecedented level. But in the decade of the 1960s a number of problems led to widespread student dissatisfaction with the very economic and political systems that had provided their opportunities for education. Such problems included: the economic and political failings of Eastern European communist states; the social and economic dislocation in noncommunist states attending a decline of traditional heavy industry and the growth of the service sector of the economy; and the protracted and costly American involvement in the Vietnam conflict.

Those problems to which the students of the 1960s demanded solutions are still timely ones that many of us highlight in our courses because they permit 1990s students better to understand the world of which they are a part. The recent breakdown of Eastern European communism can be better understood through a knowledge of the student and intellectual dissatisfaction that produced the Prague Spring of 1968. The problems of late industrial economic development and the omnipotence of the modern state were boldly protested by Paris students in 1968. And events like the American presidential campaign of 1992 can be fully comprehended by today's students only if they are aware of the internal division that the Vietnam War provoked almost three decades ago. Thus we have chosen to focus here on the issues raised by European students in the 1960s. In thus focusing this chapter we again are introducing students to new historical sources, in this case political cartoons.

The Problem

Content objectives:

1. to understand economic and social problems of the 1960s

2. to better understand the present-day West through analysis of 1960s-era problems, such as the economic failings of Eastern European communist states and the difficulties posed by late-twentieth-century industrial developments and the growth of the modern state

Skills objectives:

1. to analyze the media of modern politics in the form of political manifestos, slogans, posters, and cartoons

2. to use the results of this analysis to understand the political movements of the 1960s and the dynamics of modern politics

Sources and Method

Like Chapter 2, Chapter 14 presents students with the challenging task of understanding political ideas through their visual expressions. This time, however, students are not asked to analyze architecture and art as evidence; rather, they are offered various expressions of modern political movements, including political cartoons, posters, and slogans scrawled on walls, as well as more traditional political manifestos. This evidence should once again remind students of the diversity of sources available to historians.

This chapter emerged from a presentation on the events of 1968, using similar sources, that one of the authors made during a course on modern French history. The students' interest in the sources and success in interpreting them led us to experiment with such presentations in Western Civilization courses. We have discovered that students find these kinds of sources interesting and, with a little guidance, comprehend readily the messages the sources convey.

The chapter's central questions guide students in analyzing the sources, and the accompanying text offers the basic methodology for interpreting the political cartoons. You will probably want to provide students some further guidance, however, in generalizing what they learn in this chapter. In terms of methodology, one of our goals is to help students critically analyze the political material they encounter both in studying history and in living as citizens of late-twentieth-century America. To facilitate such critical analysis, you may wish to apply this chapter's analytical techniques to political manifestos and cartoons drawn from contemporary events. In terms of content, you might promote class discussion about the connections between 1968 and the present. Communism's recent collapse in Eastern Europe can be much better understood in view of the events of 1968. Certainly, too, the economic and political challenges of the 1990s reflect many of the basic problems raised by Paris students in 1968.

The Evidence

Students analyze several kinds of evidence in this chapter, and you may wish to reinforce their understanding of the different analytical methods they should employ. Sources 1, 2, 13, and 14 are political manifestos of the Paris and Prague opposition movements. They present few reading difficulties for students, but their message can be underlined by helping students understand the revolutionary nature of the manifestos' demands on their respective political and economic systems. French president Pompidou was quite correct in characterizing the Parisian students' movement as a revolt against much of modern society. The political slogans in Source 3, phrased in terms that allow no compromise, can be used to particularly good effect to reinforce contemporary students' understanding of the character of the 1968 student protests.

   Sources 4 through 12 and 15 through 20 present the same risk posed by other pictorial evidence in *Discovering the Western Past:* the danger that students will give such evidence only cursory attention. You may wish to highlight the analytical techniques offered in this chapter and, as we suggested earlier, generalize those techniques. Such analysis should aid students in understanding, for example, the form "capital" assumes in Source 4, the slope of the wounded De Gaulle's crutches in Source 12, and the garb of Walter Ulbricht in Source 18.

Questions To Consider

The questions posed in this section should guide students to a better understanding of the events of the late 1960s. You may profitably pose additional questions that draw many aspects of your course together. For example, you might ask students to reflect back on Chapter 6's evidence about the nature of early industrial work; then, using the 1960s French protests about working conditions as a comparison, ask students if the essential character of such labor has changed very much. In a similar way, we find that the Czechoslovakian evidence provides excellent entry, after a few additional questions from us, to the whole problem of communism's recent collapse in Eastern Europe and the Soviet Union.

Epilogue and Evaluation

As usual, the epilogue takes students beyond the issues and events presented in the chapter. This process can be particularly rewarding with this chapter's theme because it raises issues still very timely: the nature of the society and economy of the modern industrial world, and the problems that led to the recent collapse of communism from which Eastern Europe will be recovering for years.

Perhaps because of the large amount of pictorial evidence in this chapter, we often use a written assignment, asking students to put themselves in the place of a 1968 student and to recreate in an essay that individual's version of the world that year. Other forms of evaluation can also be productive. We have used a role-playing situation in which students assume the identities of 1968 students and respond to various issues. That format can provide a good mode of analysis and can also prove quite stimulating: as the 1992 American presidential campaign reminded many, we have yet to fully exorcise the demons of 1968 from our political memory.

For Further Reading

France

John Ardagh, *The New French Revolution: A Social and Economic Study of France, 1945–1968* (1968), and *France in the 1980s* (1982). The works of a perceptive British journalist on postwar France before and after De Gaulle.

Raymond Aron, *The Elusive Revolution: Anatomy of a Student Revolt* (1969). This work, by one of postwar France's most important thinkers, is critical of the students but nonetheless perceptive about the causes of the revolt.

Bernard E. Brown, *Protest in Paris: Anatomy of a Revolt* (1974). An excellent study of the problems and ideologies that led to the 1968 revolt, suggesting that the revolt was the product of rapid modernization.

David Caute, *The Year of the Barricades: A Journey Through 1968* (1988). A general history of the year's events that puts France in an international context.

Daniel and Gabriel Cohn-Bendit, *Obsolete Communism: The Left-Wing Alternative* (1968). The work of Daniel Cohn-Bendit, his brother, and other members of the student movement, this is a basic expression of the methods and goals of the student leaders.

Ronald Fraser (ed.), *1968: A Student Generation in Revolt* (1988). A history that treats France in the international context by examining the student movements in the United States, Britain, Northern Ireland, Germany, and Italy.

Richard Johnson, *The French Communist Party Versus the Students: Revolutionary Politics in May–June 1968* (1972). A study of a revolutionary party and the reasons for its avoidance of revolution in 1968.

Alain Schnapp and Pierre Vidal-Naquet (eds.), *The French Student Uprising, November 1967–June 1968* (1971). An excellent collection of documents that presents the events of 1968 in the words of participants.

Alain Touraine, *The May Movement: Revolt and Reform* (1971). A study of the French events by a sociologist at Nanterre, sympathetic to the students, who finds that a new struggle had supplanted that of workers and capitalists in the late industrial age: a struggle between a "technocratic bureaucratic class" and those whom they would control.

Czechoslovakia

Timothy Ash, *The Magic Lantern: The Revolution of '89 Witnessed in Warsaw, Budapest, Berlin, and Prague* (1990). Places Czechoslovakia's 1989 "Velvet Revolution" in the context of communism's fall in the rest of Eastern Europe.

John F. N. Bradley, *Politics in Czechoslovakia, 1945–1990* (1991). A brief but comprehensive study of Czechoslovakia since World War II.

Karel Kaplan, *The Short March: The Communist Takeover in Czechoslovakia, 1945–1948* (1987). A new study of events surrounding the communist coup of 1948, essential to understanding contemporary Czechoslovakia.

Vladimir V. Kusin, *The Intellectual Origins of the Prague Spring: The Development of Reformist Ideas in Czechoslovakia, 1956–1967* (1971). A good study of the background for the events of 1968.

Journalist "M," *A Year Is Eight Months: Czechoslovakia, 1968* (1970). Provides firsthand accounts of many of the events of 1968 by a Czech journalist.

Robin Alison Remington (ed.), *Winter in Prague: Documents on Czechoslovakian Communism in Crisis* (1969). An excellent documentary collection that includes the manifesto "Two Thousand Words" of June 1968 calling for Czechoslovakian changes to go still further.

H. Gordon Skilling, *Czechoslovakia's Interrupted Revolution* (1976). A detailed, historical account of 1968.

Tim D. Whipple (ed.), *After the Velvet Revolution: Václav Havel and the New Leaders of Czechoslovakia Speak Out* (1991). Reflections on Czechoslovakia's future and communist past by leaders including Alexander Dubček.

Z. A. B. Zeman, *Prague Spring* (1969). Another firsthand account of events in Prague, this time by a British journalist of Czech origin.

CHAPTER FIFTEEN

Europe and the Wider World in the 1990s

Many Western Civilization textbooks devote little attention to Europe's recent past. Yet significant late-twentieth-century developments have begun to reshape Europe permanently. Thus we devoted Chapter 14 to a number of the recent problems, including unrest in Eastern Europe, that have had a major impact on the continent, and in Chapter 15 we do the same. Our subject this time is the European Community, which we examine from its foundation to the present; we raise issues about the Community that will probably occupy diplomats and politicians for the rest of this decade. Will the European Community achieve further integration, especially in currency and defense policies? Will an economically more integrated Community attempt to remake itself into a "fortress Europe" that will exclude non-European goods? Will the Community expand to include all of Europe, especially former communist nations of the east? Will a prosperous Community remain open to immigrants from less prosperous, non-European nations?

The Problem

Content objectives:

1. to understand Europe's post–World War II role in the world

2. to learn about the development of the European Community and its institutions

3. to analyze current challenges to the European unity movement

Skills objectives:

1. to use several standard kinds of historical sources, including treaties and newspapers, to understand European events

2. to analyze newspaper sources for underlying editorial opinion that may shape the way a news story is presented

3. to use the sources of contemporary history to suggest the possible resolutions of current problems

Sources and Method

Chapter 15 should accomplish several goals. First, it should help students understand the reasons for the foundation of European Community institutions in the wake of World War II. You can reinforce students' understanding of the impulse toward economic unity by emphasizing the widespread destruction of European industry and transportation in the war, along with the loss of European global political influence that accompanied the rise of the American and Soviet superpowers.

The chapter should also lead students to understand the rapid recovery made by the European nations after the war, a recovery so dramatic that in Germany and Italy it is often referred to as an "economic miracle." A key concept is the role that the Common Market played in this economic rebuilding. In this regard you may wish to emphasize the most graphic evidence of the Common Market's role in recovery: the great disparity, revealed in Source 4, between the growth of industrial production in non–Common Market countries (such as Great Britain) and that in member countries.

By the time they finish this chapter, students should also be aware that future extension of European unity will come at the price of the loss of some national identity. We like to recall nineteenth-century nationalism for students while reflecting on Britain's reluctance to be integrated into a common currency union that, inevitably, would be German dominated. Traditional nationalism also manifests itself in the antiforeign movement of Jean-Marie Le Pen in France and in the protests against immigrants in eastern Germany.

The Evidence

This final chapter of *Discovering the Western Past* continues to present students with new kinds of sources for understanding the past. The documents of modern international relations, in the form of treaties and statements of policy by foreign ministers, appear here for the first time in Sources 2, 3, and 8. You may wish to emphasize the importance of such documentation in reconstructing the last several centuries of history; treaties have the force of international contracts, and they often attempt to spell out every contingency in the issues they address.

Our goal throughout *Discovering the Western Past* has been to lead students to a critical analysis of the sources. Students' experience with political cartoons in Chapter 14 should provide some foundation for close analysis of the newspaper articles in Sources 5, 6, and 10. You may wish to remind students that newspapers do have individual editorial points of view and that these may well determine how a newspaper interprets the news. You may wish to emphasize the relevance of understanding editorial opinion by contrasting, as one of us does in class discussions, the editorial viewpoints of several examples of the American press.

The rest of the sources in this chapter include memoir literature (Source 1) and statistical data (Sources 4, 7, 9, and 11) that students should already be accustomed to analyzing. You may, however, wish to reinforce the lessons of earlier chapters in analyzing such sources. For example, for Source 4, which conveys industrial production, you might profitably remind students how to interpret data that relate to a base year whose output is expressed as 100.

Questions to Consider

Because Chapter 15 explores contemporary issues in European affairs, we find that discussion of the basic questions can be amplified by discussing current issues affecting the European Community. For example, the Maastricht agreements of December 1991 pledged the Community to create a common currency, but problems soon arose because each member nation had to ratify the accords. The United Kingdom immediately held back from any integration into a common currency system. While parliaments in other member states readily ratified the agreements, difficulties arose in those nations that put the Maastricht accords to plebiscites. Danes rejected the Maastricht plan in a plebiscite, and French voters ratified their country's participation by the narrowest of margins. Such developments immediately cast doubt on Europe's continued path toward unity because, plainly, nationalism was the cause of the negative votes. As a result, your students will probably be reading in the press about a slowdown in the European drive toward greater economic unity. For the current news on this issue, the sources in Chapter 15 provide essential background.

European Community matters can also be expected to provide other opportunities for you to link class discussion of the chapter with current events.

German and French leaders seem resolved to push ahead with a program for a Community defense policy. Indeed, they already have created a Franco-German military unit. But nationalist sentiment in other nations clearly opposes such a policy, and it probably will remain a source of disagreement among European leaders. Another issue raised in this chapter will figure in the news as well: the problem of immigration into Europe from economically less developed nations. As this chapter went to press, Germany was poised to enact immigration restrictions in the face of continuing violence against immigrants. Other European nations may follow the German lead. By emphasizing the continuing process and problems of European integration, we believe you can promote the valuable kind of class discussion we generated when we tested the material with our own students.

Epilogue and Evaluation

In our epilogue, like all others in *Discovering the Western Past,* we endeavor to take students beyond the chapter itself to enhance their understanding of the broader issues posed by the chapter's sources. In classroom discussion, it is perhaps fitting for this final chapter that you build on our epilogue by drawing much of the course material together. Ask students, for example, to reflect on nationalism, drawing in part from the material in Chapters 9 and 11. Does the development of the European Community suggest that European nationalism has been modified since World War II? What do students make of such a seemingly contradictory development as the waning of traditional Franco-German antipathy at the same time that many European states, especially Germany, are experiencing expressions of antiforeign sentiments by their citizens?

Evaluation of students' mastery of this chapter may take several forms. Traditional essay questions may be employed, asking students to trace the origins and development of Community institutions and to assess the prospects of the European unity movement. A round-table discussion may provide an alternative. Divide students into national delegations for a mock meeting of the European Community. Remind them of past national antipathies and nationalist sentiments, and then set them to discussing a proposal to increase economic interdependence at the expense of national independence. Remind students, too, that each national delegation can be expected to approach the proposal with a "What's in it for us?" attitude. You then may judge how students draw on Chapter 15 to discuss the issue you have presented.

For Further Reading

Colin Crouch and David Marguand (eds.), *The Politics of 1992: Beyond the Single European Market* (1990). A collection of thoughtful essays on political issues facing the Community. Authors include Lord Cockfield, who was vice-president of the European Commission from 1985 to 1988.

Michael Emerson et al., *The Economics of 1992: The E.C. Commission's Assessment of the Economic Effects of Completing the Internal Market* (1988). A technical study highlighting the projected economic benefits of a single European market.

John Gillingham, *Coal, Steel, and the Rebirth of Europe, 1945–1955: The Germans and French from Ruhr Conflict to Economic Community* (1991). A detailed history of the origins and foundation of the European Coal and Steel Community.

Frances Nicholson and Roger East, *From Six to Twelve: The Enlargement of the European Communities* (1987). A detailed study of the negotiations to expand the EC.

Carl H. Pegg, *Evolution of the European Idea, 1914–1932* (1983). A study of the important attempts, by Aristide Briand and others, to achieve European unity between the two world wars.